The
COMPLETE
CHRISTIAN

The COMPLETE CHRISTIAN

Robert S. Wood

To Ben —
Dixie's favorite seminary
teacher! [signature] warmest wishes.
Rob S Wood

DESERET BOOK

SALT LAKE CITY, UTAH

Biblical citations are generally from the King James Version of the Bible; however, where noted, *The New English Bible with the Apocrypha* (Oxford: Oxford University Press, 1970) [NEB] is quoted.

Library of Congress Cataloging-in-Publication Data

Wood, Robert S., 1936–
    The complete Christian / Robert S. Wood.
        p. cm.
    Includes bibliographical references and index.
    ISBN-13: 978-1-59038-750-4 (hardbound : alk. paper)
    1. Christian life—Mormon authors. I. Title.
    BX8656.W623 2007
    248.4'89332—dc22   2007008321

Printed in the United States of America
R. R. Donnelley and Sons, Crawfordsville, IN

10   9   8   7   6   5   4   3   2   1

For my wife and four daughters

who demonstrate every day what it is to be

a complete Christian

"And righteousness will I send down out of heaven; and truth will I send forth out of the earth, to bear testimony of mine Only Begotten; his resurrection from the dead; yea, and also the resurrection of all men; and righteousness and truth will I cause to sweep the earth as with a flood, to gather out mine elect from the four quarters of the earth."

—MOSES 7:62

CONTENTS

Contents

PREFACE

Some years ago I was invited to attend a special session of a meeting of the Brazilian House of Deputies. The occasion provided opportunities for members of the Brazilian Congress to pay special tribute to The Church of Jesus Christ of Latter-day Saints for the positive contributions the Church was making in Brazil. One congressman after another arose and said very nice things about the Church. The presentation that stands out most prominently in my mind, however, was by one very senior member of the House. He said that he had noted that many professors of religion at Brazil's leading university had lost faith in the miracles of the Bible, including the miracle of the Resurrection. He said that a copy of the Book of Mormon had come into his hands. He reported that he had read it and had concluded that it stands as a definitive witness that the Bible is true and that Jesus did in fact rise from the dead to become the Savior of mankind.

Listening to him, I was struck again by the thought that the great work of the Restoration was to reestablish the truth of the gospel in the hearts of people everywhere and to raise anew the standard of righteousness on the earth.

This book is a reflection on how each of us establishes that truth and righteousness in our lives. If the Lord has summoned the Church out of obscurity and darkness, then as members, each of us stands as a representative of the fact that the heavens have again opened and that they resound with the glad tiding of the gospel. In every aspect of our lives we are called to develop true understanding, true character, true discipleship, and true faith.

I am grateful to Sheri Dew and Cory H. Maxwell of Deseret Book for their encouragement of this project and to Richard Peterson for his editorial work, Richard Erickson for his artistic design, and Laurie Cook for her typesetting skills. I am also indebted to my wonderful secretary, Arlene Calkins, for her wise assistance.

Truth and Righteousness in the Latter Days

Some years ago, my wife and I were privileged to participate in a meeting of the Area Authority Seventies and mission presidents and their wives who were serving in the North America Northeast Area of the Church, a gathering that extended over several days. Elder Neal A. Maxwell of the Quorum of the Twelve Apostles presided, and members of the area presidency were in attendance. We were convened in the Marriott Hotel at the Washington Dulles International Airport.

On Monday morning I had to leave my wife and the others to attend another meeting related to my work in the Pentagon. The meeting in the Pentagon was attended by senior members of the White House staff, cabinet members, and many military commanders. I remember thinking as I sat with that group what remarkable people they were—not only were they extraordinarily talented and hardworking but were both true patriots and men and women of faith. I thought to myself, *These are really good people and how lucky the nation is to have such people serving the country.*

At the conclusion of the Pentagon conference, I drove back to the Marriott Hotel to rejoin the Church meeting. As I made my way to the room where the brothers and sisters were, I was thinking about the good people with whom I had just been associating. Then something quite extraordinary happened. As I opened the door and crossed the threshold of the room where Elder Maxwell was speaking, tears welled up in my eyes, and I felt I had just crossed the boundary into the celestial kingdom! The thought occurred to me, *These are also good people; but they are something else. They are holy people.* I do not mean that they were perfect, but I do mean that they had taken seriously the divine mandate and had received the associated blessing: "Sanctify yourselves and ye shall be endowed with power, that ye may give even as I have spoken" (D&C 43:16). They were people who had a special commission, one common to all those who are part of the kingdom, raised up to establish the Lord's purposes in the latter days.

We live in the most decisive moment in human history. The very name of the Church—The Church of Jesus Christ of Latter-day Saints—points not only to Him who is our foundation but to the age in which we live and the kind of people we have covenanted to be. The "latter-days" is often designated by the Lord as "the dispensation of the fulness of times," a period in which the Lord will "gather together in one all things in Christ, both which are in heaven, and which are on earth" (Ephesians 1:10). It is in this season of the earth's history that all the promises and hopes of patriarchs and prophets in ages past will come to pass. To that end the Lord has once again reconstituted His people and summoned them to be a light to the nations and to prepare the way for His triumphant return.

The people of ancient Israel entered into a covenant with Jehovah by which He became their Lord and they became His people. The promised blessing to these covenant people was that as a consequence of their obedience to His commandments, the Lord would buoy them up in their trials and redeem them from their transgressions. Only if they accepted Him as Lord and Master could He be their Redeemer. Hence, the Lord speaking through Moses said to them:

> Now therefore, if ye will obey my voice indeed, and keep my covenant, then ye shall be a peculiar treasure unto me above all people: for all the earth is mine: And ye shall be unto me a kingdom of priests, and an holy nation. [Exodus 19:5–6]

With the new covenant established during the Lord's earthly ministry, believers were summoned as was ancient Israel into a special relationship. As Peter declared of the Saints of his day:

> But ye are a chosen generation, a royal priesthood, an holy nation, a peculiar people; that ye should shew forth the praises of him who hath called you out of darkness into his marvellous light: Which in time past were not a people, but are now the people of God. [1 Peter 2:9–10]

Once again, this time in latter days, the Lord has constituted a covenant people, counseling holiness and mandating them as the righteous leaven for all peoples. The *"weight of glory"* now rests on the Latter-day Saints. As with ancient Israel and the former-day Saints, a general covenant has been made constituting a people—members of The Church of Jesus Christ of Latter-day Saints—to be the leaven and the agent of change in the course of history and in the lives of all mankind. When each of us is baptized, we are made a party to that covenant.

In the temple, we specify explicitly the terms of that covenant. We pledge to live a life of sacrifice, of consecration, and of Christlike service and demeanor. As Christ has done, we agree to submit our will to that of the Father, standing with Christ in working to bring to pass the exaltation of mankind and devoting our all to the establishment of the kingdom of God upon the earth. We lose our life for Christ's sake, and as a consequence, gain not only the establishment of Zion but our own eternal lives.

In His great intercessory prayer, offered by Jesus just prior to His betrayal and arrest, the Lord described the divine partnership in these words: "Neither pray I for these [the Apostles] alone, but for them also which shall believe on me through their word; That they all may be one; as thou, Father, art in me, and I in thee, that they also may be one in us: that the world may believe that thou hast sent me" (John 17:20–21). If we are not one with the Godhead and united with each other, we are, as Christ declared, not His (see Matthew 7:21–23).

Our Face of Battle and the Eternal Stakes

John Keegan, a military historian, commenting on what he called "the face of battle," noted that the individual soldier often never sees the course of the battle itself or comprehends the full scale of the broader war of which the battle is a part.[1] Hunkered down in his personal foxhole, often beset by fatigue and feelings of isolation and unable to grasp the full dimensions of the conflict, he fails to see that implicit in his personal struggle lie the shaking of kingdoms and the fate of nations.

So it is with us who have entered into sacred covenant with our Heavenly Father and have become part of a people with a mandate to bear one another's burdens and to alter the course of history. Only if we grasp the eternal stakes involved will we be able to make sense of our own individual and family "face of battle." Such a sense will help us define how we should deal with the daily irritations and problems of life, including our fellow warriors, who, like us, are imperfect. Most important, having a sense of the great cause of which we are part, we can put our own imperfections in perspective. Brigham Young understood this:

> Except I am one with my good brethren, do not say that I am a Latter-day Saint. We must be one. Our faith must be concentrated in one great work—the building up of the Kingdom of God on the earth, and our works must aim at the accomplishment of that great purpose.
>
> We have got to be united in our efforts. We should go to work with a united faith like the heart of one man; and whatever we do should be performed in the name of the Lord, and we will then be blessed and prospered in all we do. We have a work on hand whose magnitude can hardly be told.
>
> It is also our duty to love the Gospel and the spirit of the Gospel, so that we can become one in the Lord, not out of Him, that our faith, our affections for truth, the kingdom of heaven, our acts, all our labor will be concentrated in the salvation of the children of men and the establishment of the Kingdom of God on the earth. This is cooperation on a very large scale. This is the work of redemption that is entered into by the Latter-day Saints. Unitedly we perform these duties, we stand, we endure, we increase and multiply, we strengthen and spread abroad, and shall continue so to do until the kingdoms of this world are the kingdoms of our God and His Christ.[2]

Having such a sense of the eternal stakes will protect us from the treachery of indifference, of murmuring, of withdrawal, and of active defiance. With such a sense, we will understand the meaning and cost of discipleship.

Through the ages the Lord has often lodged a serious complaint against His people, which is that they have forgotten that they, "which in times past were not a people, but are now the people of God," take lightly their divine commission and fail as individuals to connect their personal lives to the great cause of which they are a part.

To ancient Israel the Lord declared that they had "lightly esteemed the Rock of his salvation" and had "forgotten [that] God that formed thee" (Deuteronomy 32:15, 18). And to modern Israel, the Latter-day Saints, the Lord complained that "your minds in times past have been darkened because of unbelief, and because you have treated lightly the things you have received." On the other hand, the Lord invites our fidelity and promises us, "Unto you who now hear my words, which are my voice, blessed are ye inasmuch as you receive these things; For I will forgive you of your sins with this commandment—that you remain steadfast in your minds in solemnity and the spirit of prayer, in bearing testimony to all the world of those things which are communicated unto you" (D&C 84:54, 60–61).

As with ancient Israel, so with the Lord's latter-day people, too often we forget in "normal times" the extraordinary charge that we have been given to bring forth and establish the cause of Zion. The Lord therefore declares: "In the day of their peace they esteemed lightly my counsel; but, in the day of their trouble, of necessity they feel after me" (D&C 101:8).

It is in this context that we can understand the Lord's

exhortation to take seriously, serious things and to make certain we are fully engaged in His eternal work.

PERSONAL QUESTS AND DIVINE PURPOSES

I have always been impressed by the questions that the young man Joseph Smith asked in 1820 and 1823—and by the dramatic nature of the answers he received. In the spring of 1820, Joseph was concerned as to which church he should join, and in September 1823, he was seeking forgiveness for all his "sins and follies" while wondering about his "state and standing" before the Lord (Joseph Smith–History 1:29). Not only did God respond to his inquiries, but in each case used those youthful concerns to facilitate the restoration of the gospel and the reestablishment of His kingdom upon the earth.

In the marvelous First Vision, the Father and the Son answered Joseph's inquiry about which church to join by informing him that the creeds of all existing sects were inadequate. Joseph soon learned that his "telling the story" of that vision made him the subject of ridicule and persecution, something he understood were the consequences of him becoming "a disturber and an annoyer" of Satan's kingdom (Joseph Smith–History 1:19).

Likewise, Moroni responded to Joseph's prayer by disclosing the existence of a sacred record containing the fulness of the gospel and announcing the commencement of a truly marvelous work and wonder by saying: "Behold, I will reveal unto you the Priesthood, by the hand of Elijah the prophet, before the coming of the great and dreadful day of the Lord. And he shall plant in the hearts of the children the promises made to the fathers, and the hearts of the children shall turn to their fathers. If it were not so, the whole earth would be utterly wasted at his coming" (D&C 2:1–3).

As with the soldier in the front lines of combat, Joseph was at first focused on his own personal battle, but the Lord expanded his peripheral vision to encompass the great latter-day struggle through which all the purposes of creation itself would reach their climax and fulfillment. Nearing the conclusion of his remarkable ministry and contemplating all that was coming to fruition as in fulfillment of the glorious visions of 1820 and 1823, Joseph was led to exclaim, "Brethren, shall we not go on in so great a cause?" (D&C 128:22).

In a real sense, the life of the Prophet Joseph Smith is a model. Just as he grew in faith and spiritual stature, "line upon line, precept on precept" (D&C 98:12), so is each of us a work in process, a bundle of hopes and fears, of noble accomplishments and base failures. But we must never lose sight of what we are to be. As Latter-day Saints, we have been called as kingdom-builders. We are part of a people crafted by divine providence and given the charge that echoes from ancient days: "For I am the Lord your God: ye shall therefore sanctify yourselves, and ye shall be holy; for I am holy" (Leviticus 11:44).

From the beginning, the prophets have taught the laws of heaven and the principles of the priesthood whereby God's people, even while living in the midst of the world, can be on holy ground. This holy realm is a social order, described in the scriptures as a kingdom—but a kingdom governed not by the principles of earthly realms nor under the direction of a worldly sovereign but by the inspiration of divine precepts and under the authority of Christ.

All of us are and should be loyal citizens of two kingdoms: the secular political communities into which the earth is divided and the transcendent kingdom of God by which the earth is united. Whether in the one kingdom or the other, however, we as Latter-day Saints should stand as witnesses of Christ in our thoughts, our words, and our actions. As Christ prayed for his apostles—and for us:

> I pray not that thou shouldest take them out of the world, but that thou shouldest keep them from the evil. They are not of the world, even as I am not of the world. Sanctify them through thy truth: thy word is truth. As thou hast sent me into the world, even so have I also sent them into the world. And for their sakes I sanctify myself, that they also might be sanctified through the truth. Neither pray I for these alone, but for them also which shall believe on me through their word. [John 17:15–20]

THE TRIALS AND GLORIES OF THE LATTER DAYS

We live in an age of fulfillment and glorious revelation. The Lord said to the Prophet Joseph Smith in Liberty Jail that the time had come when "God shall give unto you knowledge by his Holy Spirit, yea, by the unspeakable gift of the Holy Ghost, that has not been revealed since the world was until now; Which our fore-fathers have awaited with anxious expectation to be revealed in the last times, which their minds were pointed to by the angels, as held in reserve for the fulness of their glory; A time to come in the which nothing shall be withheld" (D&C 121:26–28).

This promise is made to those who, the Lord declared, "serve me in righteousness and in truth unto the end. Great shall be their reward and eternal shall be their glory. And to them will I reveal all mysteries, yea, all the hidden mysteries of my kingdom from days of old, and for ages to come, will I make known unto them the good pleasure of my will concerning all things pertaining to my kingdom" (D&C 76:5–7).

Surely this is a marvelous time to be alive! But, if we live in an age of glorious light, it is also a day of profound darkness. If it is a time of breathtaking endowment of understanding and power from on high, it is as well an epoch of unparalleled wickedness. Perhaps to no one was this revealed more vividly than to the ancient prophet Enoch, as recorded in Moses 7. The Lord told Enoch that in a day to come, the wickedness of the world would culminate in the great flood, but that a remnant, the family of Noah, would be preserved. However, the evil that the flood would cut short would rise once again (see vv. 42–43).

Lamenting this awful scene, Enoch cried out in anguish, "When shall the day of the Lord come? When shall the blood of the Righteous be shed [referring to the atoning sacrifice of Christ], that all they that mourn may be sanctified and have eternal life?" (v. 45)

The Lord replied, "It shall be in the 'meridian of time.'" But He added the ominous note that the mortal ministry of the Lord would be "in the days of wickedness and vengeance" (v. 46).

Insistently, Enoch asked if the earth would ever rest and be free of such filthiness. The Lord, looking forward to His return as the triumphant, resurrected Lord, answered yes. But again, the last days preceding this glorious consummation would be "days of wickedness and vengeance." Indeed, "the heavens shall be darkened, and a veil of darkness shall cover the earth; and the heavens shall shake, and also the earth; and great tribulations shall be among the children of men" (see vv. 54–61).

Enoch was given to understand that both the dispensation of the meridian of time and the dispensation of the last days were to be eras of miracles and redemptive power—but they were also to be days of unspeakable depravity. This appears to be the "normal" state of mother earth, who in Enoch's vision cried out, "I am pained, I am weary, because of the wickedness of my children. When shall I rest, and be cleansed from the filthiness which is gone forth out of me?" (v. 48). In one of the most chilling images ever recorded, the scriptures say: "And [Enoch] beheld Satan; and he had a great chain in his hand, and it veiled the whole face of the earth with darkness; and he looked up and laughed, and his angels rejoiced" (v. 26).

It is important that we who have been summoned forth, like the inhabitants of Enoch's Zion, understand how important it is that we remain unspotted from this world, that we may cause the kingdom of God to roll forth, even in a day of wickedness and vengeance. As the seeds of apostasy began to sprout in his day, the Apostle Paul defined the nature of the struggle. He wrote, "We wrestle not against flesh and blood, but against principalities, against powers, against the rulers of the darkness of this world, against spiritual wickedness in high places" (Ephesians 6:12).

Paul was pointing to an important phenomenon. The problem was not to merely counter individual cases of transgression but to resist an entire system of wickedness. It was the same condition described by Isaiah in his day (see Isaiah 24:5) and by the Lord in 1831, when He revealed the following to Joseph Smith:

> For they have strayed from mine ordinances, and have broken mine everlasting covenant; They seek not the Lord to establish his righteousness, but every man walketh in his own way, and after the image of his own god, whose image is in the likeness of the world, and whose substance is that of an idol, which waxeth old and shall perish in

Babylon, even Babylon the great, which shall fall. [D&C 1:15–16]

This condition is technically referred to as corruption, which literally means to debase and to change good to bad. In a real sense, a corrupt society calls good bad and bad good. Those who are molded by such a society literally do not understand what is correct and ignorantly pursue ignoble goals.

Writing four hundred years before the birth of Christ, the Greek philosopher Plato brilliantly described the nature of a corrupt society. Plato argued that there is an interconnectedness between what he called the constitution or regime of a society and the character of the people who are members of that society. By constitution, he included not only the written or unwritten code regulating power but the general ways in which society is arranged—its ways of persuading, educating, and entertaining; the ways and reasons for which people are rewarded or penalized; the general patterns of influence; people's expectations of each other; and what is considered shameful or honorable. As he observed, "There must be as many types of human character as there are forms of government. Constitutions cannot come out of stock and stones; they must result from the preponderance of certain characters which draw the rest of the community in their wake."[3]

If the community is corrupted, that corruption will first come from those who are the entrusted leaders and models of the society, that is, those who exercise political and social power and who set the tone and direction of the community. In time, the people as a whole will exhibit the vices of their leaders, for therein will they perceive acceptance and rewards and escape the ridicule of "listening to a different drummer."

Plato argued that the decline of society is closely associated with changes in the regulation of marriage and childbirth. Elite attitudes, finally reflected in law concerning the family, will powerfully determine the kind of society and the type of dominant personality that emerges. Associated with these transformations will be the rise of artistic expressions—music, drama, comedy, entertainment—that will subject old values to contempt and establish new sets of values. He asserted that artistic expression may be the most powerful tool in shaping the people's "souls" and the nature of society.[4]

The deterioration of liberty into license and the collapse of self-discipline leads at last, observed Plato, to despotism. As he wrote:

> Law-abiding citizens will be insulted as nonentities who hug their chains. . . . In such a state the spirit of liberty is bound to go to all lengths. . . . The citizens become so sensitive that they resent the slightest application of control as intolerable tyranny, and in their resolve to have no master, they end by disregarding even the law, written or unwritten. . . . The truth is that, in the constitution of society, quite as much as in the weather or in plants and animals, any excess brings about an equally violent reaction. So the only outcome of too much freedom is likely to be excessive subjugation, in the state or in the individual; which means that the culmination of liberty in democracy is precisely what prepares the way for the cruelest extreme of servitude under a despot.[5]

Thucydides, a contemporary of Plato, gives in his account of the fortunes and fall of the empire of democratic Athens, a chilling perspective on the violence and savagery into which the cities of Greece had sunk. Unrestrained passions, fraud, greed, and unspeakable brutality were rampant. Simple devotion to principle and an uncomplicated adherence to duty were, he wrote, ridiculed. Reliance on divine commands was replaced by "attractive arguments to justify some disgraceful action," and the "ordinary conventions of civilized life [were] thrown into confusion. Human nature, always ready to offend even where laws exist, showed itself proudly in its true colors, as something incapable of controlling passion, insubordinate to the idea of justice, the enemy to anything superior to itself." Men in their behavior began to disregard the "general laws of humanity."[6]

Mormon, like Thucydides, a commander of his people and the author-editor of the record of their fortunes, writes an even more compelling tale of the rise and fall of civilized life: "O the depravity of my people! They are without order and without mercy. Behold, I am but a man, and I have but the strength of a man, and I cannot any longer enforce my commands. And they have become strong in their perversion; and they are alike brutal, sparing none, neither old nor young; and they delight in everything save that which is good; . . . they are without principle, and past feeling." The most horrendous impact, noted Mormon, was on the family: the suffering of the women and the children was indescribable. He concludes that he could not recommend his people unto God, for he knew, as he wrote, "They must perish except they repent and return unto him" (Moroni 9:18–22).

How do a society and its members sink into such depravity? Step by step. And, in the first instance, among those whose position and privilege give them particular responsibility for setting the tone of the community. As Isaiah observed, "For the leaders of this people cause them to err; and they that are led of them are destroyed" (Isaiah 9:16). The fates of the ancient Greeks and of the descendants of Lehi are but cautionary tales, perhaps even types or shadows, for our society.

We live in the age of the great divide—an ever broadening gap between the values that the Lord has declared as the foundation of His Church and kingdom and the values of society as a whole. But it would be naive to believe that we who count ourselves as citizens of His Church and kingdom are untouched by the profane perspectives that permeate our culture. In music, in art, in literature, in recreation, in law, in politics, in social practice—in all and through all—the spirit of anti-Christ pervades ever more brazenly. So destructive is this spirit that the mortal Messiah declared, "And except those days should be shortened, there should no flesh be saved: but for the elect's sake those days shall be shortened" (Matthew 24:22).

What then are the central characteristics of corruption or, in the words of the Lord, societies of wickedness and vengeance? Three elements stand out: (1) faulty understanding, (2) weak or ignoble commitments, and (3) trivial pursuits.

Paul described the depraved of his day as "having [their] understanding darkened, being alienated from the life of God through the ignorance that is in them, because of the blindness of their heart" (Ephesians 4:18). Too many people, in the words of the Doctrine and Covenants, no longer walk in the light of understanding because of "disobedience and the tradition of their fathers" (D&C 93:39). In contemporary parlance, they just don't get it. Asking the wrong questions and seeking enlightenment from the wrong sources, they never arrive at what is true. Again, as Paul observed, they are "ever learning, and never able to come to the knowledge of the truth" (2 Timothy 3:7).

Corrupt ages also see either a weakening of firm commitments or commitments to that which degrades. Most people in such an age both too readily make professions of fidelity and loyalty and abandon them as circumstances or sentiments change. Others make commitments to each other to advance ignoble causes. They become conspirators in unrighteousness, as were the Gadianton robbers described in the Book of Mormon, who "spread the works of darkness and abominations over all the face of the land, until [they] dragged the people down to an entire destruction" (Helaman 6:28). Alas, we too often see, on the one hand, people of empty promises or, on the other, those of deranged fanaticism.

Finally, in a corrupt age many do not willfully choose evil but simply fail to embrace good. They are effectively so distracted by trivial pursuits that they miss the weightier things. Elder Neal A. Maxwell once remarked that "we can easily find ourselves anxiously engaged in doing . . . lesser things, so that too little of ourselves and of our time are left over for the things of God."[7] The Lord has urgently counseled that "men should be anxiously engaged in a good cause, and do many things of their own free will, and bring to pass much righteousness. For the power is in them, wherein they are agents unto themselves" (D&C 58:27–28).

Faulty understanding, weak or perverted commitments, and busy engagement in lesser things—how are these spiritual defects reflected in the views of contemporary society? What are some of the patterns of corruption? I would mention only six:

1. **Sexual liberation, gender roles, and the family.** The retreat from moral standards governing sexual behavior, the blurring of gender roles, and the assault on the family are all of one piece. Over the last century, sexual practices have become increasingly detached from procreation and have come to be seen as recreational activities governed by "taste" rather than any moral absolutes. At the same time, the social roles of men and women have also come to be viewed as purely discretionary. The extension of these perspectives to homosexual practice and the

definition of the family are but logical outcomes of the so-called "sexual revolution." Increased tolerance of sexual relations outside the bonds of marriage in heterosexual practice was bound to be extended to other behavior that had previously been defined as abnormal or perverse.

2. Entertainment. In their depictions of society, contemporary music, art, literature, drama, television, and movies have increasingly legitimized immoral behavior and become an engine for the lowering of expectations and standards in personal responsibility, individual integrity, sexual behavior, and family life. "Normal" has been redefined in people's minds, and "tolerance" has evolved into acceptance and legitimization. The identification of the "good guys" and the "bad guys" is turned upside down, and that which was once considered noble and heroic is now cast as retrograde and bigoted.

3. Civil society and politics. In our time the original understanding of the legitimate basis for rule, as enunciated in the Declaration of Independence, the U. S. Constitution, and traditional practice has been transformed into the radical assertion that each individual is the measure of the validity of personal pursuits and relationships. In contemporary terms, policy arguments are often framed in terms of the right to direct one's life in pursuit of an individually-determined definition of happiness, which may be sought either in solitary fashion or in conjunction with others as long as it is done by mutual consent. The only limitation on this right is the maintenance of public order or security from violence.

In practical terms, this implies that institutions, such as the family, and the definition of virtue and vice are but social constructions that may vary over time and even from individual to individual or group to group. In effect, within increasingly broad parameters, acceptable social activities are simply justified by the mutual consent of the parties concerned and the claim that there is no direct damage to the security of the community. No moral reasoning is required.

The state is expected to be largely agnostic as to the different "lifestyles" of its people and to ensure that public privilege or benefits do not favor one manner of living over another but are "fairly" granted to all. For instance, see the current argument that if there are to be certain benefits accorded to traditionally defined families, then any domestic partnership must receive those same benefits.

In this construction, the political community is solely designed to secure the rights of the individual by maintaining physical security and by enforcing an equality of values so that moral reprobation is reserved only for those who believe that there *is* a hierarchy of values that should be reflected in public policy. To the degree that the state may still be seen as a moral community, it is only so at the lowest common denominator.

4. **Corporate governance, business and labor practices, and personal honesty.** The imperative to tell the truth, be it in the boardroom or the classroom, has diminished to the point that executives and pupils alike see honesty only as an instrumental value; that is, be honest only to the extent that it serves one's immediate self-interest. Contracts are no longer shaped by the rule that commitments are to be kept but by the norm that the continuance of commitments depends on circumstance.

5. **Violence in thought, language, and actions.** As norms of propriety, deference, and distinction are eroded, a kind of "in-your-face" climate grows in day-to-day social intercourse. Daily incivility is quickly translated into an indifference to others, then cruelty, and finally violence. Violence in the home and in the

street may grow more out of the soil of crudeness and rudeness than out of economic circumstances.

6. The widening gap between the "haves" and the "have-nots." The issue here is not the inequality of conditions incident to any free and open society, but the unseemly accumulation of wealth at any cost and insensitivity to both justice and mercy on the part of the "haves" and the envy and similar loosening of moral constraints on the part of the "have-nots."

It is recorded in Moses that the Lord wept over the corruption of His children. Having seen the great depravity through the ages and into the latter days revealed to him by the Lord, Enoch also wept. Prophets and apostles have anguished over men and women, whole societies, who are without God in the world. President Gordon B. Hinckley observed, "We live in a season when fierce men do terrible and despicable things. We live in a season of war. We live in a season of arrogance. We live in a season of wickedness, pornography, immorality. All of the sins of Sodom and Gomorrah haunt our society. Our young people have never faced a greater challenge. We have never seen more clearly the lecherous face of evil."[8] But, President Hinckley has also declared, "Notwithstanding the great evil of these times, what a glorious season it has been and now is. A new day has come in the work of the Almighty."[9]

We have been considering the darkness of the world. We must return to the light also coming into the world—and our role as children of the light. In familiar hymns, we sing, "The morning breaks, the shadows flee,"[10] and, "The Spirit of God like a fire is burning! The latter-day glory begins to come forth."[11] Let us consider again the vision opened up to Enoch. Having detailed the great corruption of the earth, the Lord then declared:

. . . but my people will I preserve; And righteousness will I send down out of heaven; and truth will I send forth out of the earth, to bear testimony of mine Only Begotten; his resurrection from the dead; yea, and also the resurrection of all men; and righteousness and truth will I cause to sweep the earth as with a flood, to gather out mine elect from the four quarters of the earth. [Moses 7:61, 62]

In all ages men and women have sought to discern the signs of the times. These signs, however, are not to be discerned in the darkness. War and rumors of war, wickedness and vengeance, have prevailed in most epochs. The true signs are seen elsewhere. When the Pharisees and the Sadducees asked the Lord for a sign from heaven as to His person and mission, He responded, "A wicked and adulterous generation seeketh after a sign; and there shall no sign be given unto it, but the sign of the prophet Jonas" (Matthew 16:4). The sign of Jonas was, of course, that he was "in the belly of the fish three days and three nights" and then came forth (Jonah 1:17). So too with the Lord, the sign of His divine Sonship would be demonstrated on the morning of the Resurrection. *This* was the sign of the meridian of time. Similarly, when they inquired of Jesus as to the signs of the last days, He described the wars and rumors of wars, the natural disasters, the great Apostasy, and the deceptions that would occur. But, He said, "For all these things must come to pass, but the end is not yet." Then He declared *the* sign of the latter day: "And this gospel of the kingdom shall be preached in all the world for a witness unto all nations; and then shall the end come" (Matthew 24:3–15). If the Resurrection was the defining sign of the meridian of time, so then, the Restoration of the gospel and kingdom and its spread throughout the world is to be the sign of "the dispensation of the fulness of times."

The prophet of our time, President Gordon B. Hinckley, has summoned us to become holy and to put aside lesser things and to join in the great cause of the Restoration: "We have become as a great army. We are now a people of consequence. Our voice is heard when we speak up. We have demonstrated our strength in meeting adversity. Our strength is our faith in the Almighty. No cause under the heavens can stop the work of God. Adversity may raise its ugly head. The world may be troubled with wars and rumors of wars, but this cause will go forward."[12] As did the Apostle Paul in the meridian of time, so a latter-day apostle calls upon us to take upon us "the whole armour of God, that [we] may be able to withstand in the evil day, and having done all, to stand" (Ephesians 6:13).

In the chapters that follow, we shall consider four dimensions of the divine armor that will enable us to withstand the darkness of the world and stand as a beacon and guide to countless individuals and families who seek the light but know not where to find it.

True Understanding
True Character
True Discipleship
True Faith

It must be acknowledged that we stand at one of the great crossroads of history. Given the strength of the adversary, never before has there been such a need for a people "of power, and of love, and of a sound mind" (2 Timothy 1:7). As never before in history, we must strive to know and be sanctified by the truth, to be true and faithful, to edify others and build Zion, and to rest our faith squarely on the Lord of time and eternity. As we do this, we shall, as did Christ, grow from grace to grace. As the Lord declared, "For if you keep my commandments you shall receive of [the Father's] fulness, and be glorified in me as I am in the Father; therefore, I say unto you, you shall receive grace for grace" (D&C 93:20).

As we contemplate all the times in which we might have lived, I think we would conclude that this is the great season of the earth. C. S. Lewis concluded his *Chronicles of Narnia* with the book *The Final Battle*. In a very real sense, we are the warriors engaged in the final battle. Never have the forces of evil been arrayed in such terrifying power, but never has the strength of truth and righteousness been more formidable. The kingdom of God has "come forth out of the wilderness of darkness, and [is shining] forth fair as the moon, clear as the sun, and terrible as an army with banners" (D&C 109:73). The trumpet has never been sounded more clearly. It is now for us to gird ourselves for battle.

PART ONE
TRUE UNDERSTANDING

———•———

Sanctified by the Truth

In the great intercessory prayer that Jesus offered for His apostles, He asked the Father to "Sanctify them through thy truth: thy word is truth" (John 17:17). Truth and righteousness are intimately linked. How we live flows from and contributes to what we know to be true. As a matter of urgency, the prophets and apostles have always invited the people to come to a knowledge and testimony of the most fundamental truths of existence. The overarching task of withstanding the evils of the world and standing unwavering in the winds of change is to *know and be sanctified by the truth*.

Born in Leicestershire, England, in 1827, John Jacques joined the Church in 1845 and commenced himself doing missionary work in his native land. In 1856, he migrated to the United States where he joined the ill-fated Martin handcart company. Before the rescue of the Martin and Willie companies on the snow-swept plains of Wyoming, he lost his eldest daughter. From 1869 to 1871, he served again as a missionary in England and later became assistant Church historian.[13]

Why did this noble man abandon his home, undertake with his family the rigors of a handcart journey to the Great Basin, and raise his voice throughout his life to proclaim the gospel? In a word, because he had discovered the *Truth.* There are many things that are true, but John Jacques not only posed the question that Pilate put to Christ, "What is truth?" but pursued the query to include: What is the nature of the universe? Does life have *a* purpose beyond the multiple and diverse goals that each of us pursues? Is there a god? If so, what is the nature of that god? What is man's relationship to Deity, and what is man's destiny? The answers to such inquiries transcend time and space. They are not limited to a particular culture or historical period. Above all things, having discovered *the* truth, one's life is dramatically changed, as was John Jacques's, who found that truth in the restored gospel of Jesus Christ. That discovery and his commitment to it, above all things, explain the choices and the actions of his life.

Exhilarated by this discovery, John Jacques wrote the eloquent words of what became one of the great hymns of the Restoration, "Oh Say, What Is Truth?" The poet answered his own query:

> *'Tis the fairest gem*
> *That the riches of worlds can produce, . . .*
> *'Tis the last and the first,*
> *For the limits of time it steps o'er.*
> *Tho the heavens depart and the earth's fountains*
> *burst,*
> *Truth, the sum of existence, will weather the*
> *worst,*
> *Eternal, unchanged, evermore.* [14]

Many times over the years, I have met people who, like John

Jacques, have been brought up short by the realization that there is something that endures beyond the passing mores, philosophies, and practices of the time—and defines what is true and right. Often, this understanding transforms not only their thinking but also their lives.

In the mid-1980s I participated in a series of discussions between officials from the Soviet Union, the United Kingdom, and the United States. The subject of the talks was the possibility of naval cooperation between America, Britain, and Russia. This happened at a time when the USSR was undergoing massive social transformations, indeed, far beyond what we then understood. The negotiations took place in all three countries.

On one occasion we were meeting in the United States. All three delegations were housed together in a conference center, where our discussions also took place. One evening I went out for a walk. Upon returning to the hotel, I discovered the head of the Soviet delegation, looking very pensive, sitting alone in a lobby area lighted only by a single table lamp. I didn't know whether or not I should disturb him, but he invited me to join him. Then began a conversation that I shall never forget.

He said to me, "The great difficulties we are now facing in the Soviet Union are really not economic or political in character. They are in fact spiritual. All the 'gods' whom we have worshipped have failed us and we know not where to turn. Dr. Wood, have you ever heard of an American prophet by the name of Joseph Smith?"

As you can imagine, I was taken aback by the question! I answered that yes, indeed I had, told him of my membership in the Church, and inquired why he asked. He said that his mother, who lived in Leningrad (now St. Petersburg), had met some representatives of the Church from Finland. They had given her a book, written in English, to read, and she had passed it on to him. He had read it while in the airplane coming over to the United States from Moscow. The book was by Elder LeGrand Richards and was entitled *A Marvelous Work and a Wonder.* He then said, "Now that I know you are a Latter-day Saint, let me see if I have grasped the key concept of this book." He then gave a remarkable exposition of Elder Richards's thesis.

He began, "As I understand it, Joseph Smith brought together two ideas that are generally in conflict with each other and combined them in a remarkable synthesis. On the one hand, the Latter-day Saints believe that mortality is but a moment in eternity and that men and women do not spring into existence at birth and are annihilated at death. We existed before birth and shall persist after death. Moreover, there is a link between those who are yet to be born, those who now live, and those who have passed beyond the grave; there is, in fact, communication across those seeming barriers. Some who have lived have returned and communicated with the living, and there is a great cooperative enterprise that links the unborn, the living, and the dead, aimed at their mutual salvation and perfection. You're mystics."

I answered that, while I was uncomfortable with the word *mystic,* his summary was quite accurate.

He then continued. "At the same time, the Latter-day Saints seem very concerned with improving the lot of mankind in mortality. They do not believe that happiness is simply for another world but needs to be established here through common temporal as well as spiritual efforts. You seem to be community builders. You're very pragmatic as well."

I replied that he had correctly concluded. He then exclaimed, using words that clearly resonated with me, "Praise be to the man who brought forth such concepts! Such ideas are the salvation of my people."

I told him that I had another book that he needed to read. In the trunk of my automobile I had a small box filled with a Russian edition of the Book of Mormon. Knowing I was going to be with a gathering of communists, one of my daughters had given the books to me and said, "Maybe you can find the occasion to distribute some of these!" Well, clearly, if ever there was such a moment, it had come. I retrieved a copy from my car and presented it to this man who was posing once again the age-old question, "Oh say, what is truth?"

The Apostle Paul counseled the Romans to be transformed by the renewal of their minds; that is, changed according to true understanding. The transformation associated with the discovery of the truth has been variously described as a liberation and a mighty change of heart. Ultimately, the inquiry after truth compels us to transcend the ephemeral values of the particular society and culture of which we are a part. It invites us to participate in the life of the divine.

In the mid-eighties, little did I think that in a few years the question that had changed John Jacques's life would so affect the life of this Russian official as well as countless numbers of his countrymen. The two chapters that follow are intended to explain how we come to know *the* truth and demonstrate how that knowledge transforms lives.

CHAPTER 1

Be Ye Transformed by the Renewal of Your Mind

When I was sixteen years old, I remember returning home early one Friday evening from a social activity, very much awake and not ready to go to bed. I thought of going outside to bounce the basketball but knew that the neighbors would not appreciate my doing so, since they probably *were* in bed. I also thought I might play some music on my phonograph but knew my parents, whose bedroom was below mine, would likely not appreciate it.

Lying on my bed stand was a copy of the Book of Mormon that my mother had placed there in the hope that I would read it. At that time, I had read *in* the Book of Mormon but had not really *read* the Book of Mormon. Indeed, the only phrase I remembered from the book was "I, Nephi, having been born of goodly parents." That evening, having not much motive beyond having nothing better to do, I began to read the Book of Mormon.

The next morning at 11:00 A.M., I was still reading. Since it was a Saturday and I didn't have to be at work until that afternoon, my parents assumed I was sleeping in. I was, however, very much awake. I was just finishing the book and reading the words of Moroni: "Yea, come unto Christ, and be perfected in him, and deny yourselves of all ungodliness; and if ye shall deny yourself of all ungodliness, and love God with all your might, mind and strength, then is his grace sufficient for you . . ." (Moroni 10:32). After closing the book I knelt by my bed and put to the test the promise Moroni had made earlier in that concluding chapter: "And when ye shall receive these things, I would exhort you that ye would ask God, the Eternal Father, in the name of Christ, if these things are not true; and if ye shall ask with a sincere heart, with real intent, having faith in Christ, he will manifest the truth of it unto you, by the power of the Holy Ghost" (Moroni 10:4).

That Saturday morning I asked for a confirmation, and I received it more clearly and powerfully than any experimental conclusion or rational deduction that I have ever made. That sure witness of the Holy Ghost became the foundation on which rest the most important convictions I hold.

The following Monday morning at school, I ran into a good friend, not a member of the Church, with whom I had many discussions about the gospel. He told me that he had a list of fifty Book of Mormon anachronisms, which demonstrated that the Book of Mormon is not based upon an ancient text but was in fact a nineteenth-century fabrication. (An anachronism refers to a person or event or thing that is chronologically out of place, a bit like saying that Julius Caesar drove his SUV into Rome.)

Well, I told my friend that he was too late, for I had received a certain witness of the Book of Mormon! But, I said to him, "Give me your list, and I will keep it." I did keep that list, and over the years, as more research and study were done by various analysts and academics, one item after the other dropped off the list. Finally, a few years ago, I was speaking to a group at Cornell

University and mentioned my list and noted that after these many years only one unexplained item remained—but that I could wait for it to be resolved. After my presentation, a distinguished professor came up to me and said, "Well, you can scratch that last item off your list." He then told me of some studies that had put to rest that remaining seeming anachronism.

Think for a minute how different my life would have been had my testimony of the Book of Mormon depended on the resolution of those fifty concerns. I have often said that, when it comes to the most fundamental truths, I have no doubts, although I may have some questions! But there are some things for which we must have a certitude that transcends our incomplete understanding and present lack of knowledge. Moroni has given us the key to understanding sacred things and prescribed how we can receive a testimony of both the most fundamental beliefs and the most sublime truths.

On January 11, 2003, in the First Worldwide Leadership Training Meeting, President Boyd K. Packer of the Quorum of the Twelve Apostles called upon our leaders to "measure everything you learn about your ordination and calling against fundamental truths"[15] and outlined those truths. Among them are the divine mission of Jesus Christ and the Church He established; the loss of the precious truths of the gospel, the changing of the ordinances, and the loss of the apostolic keys in the Apostasy; the Restoration under the direction of the Father and the Son and through the Prophet Joseph Smith of that which had been lost; and the continuation of the apostolic and priesthood keys in the Church today.

President Packer pointed to the Holy Ghost as the sextant that each individual receives at baptism in order to discern and establish in our lives these truths. Elder Neal A. Maxwell, also of the

Quorum of the Twelve Apostles, similarly addressed our responsibility to receive personal revelation that each of us may have a sure witness of those fundamental truths.

What exactly *is* the nature of the truth of revelation and the witness of the Spirit?

FROM INFORMATION TO KNOWLEDGE

We are said to be living in the midst of an information revolution. We have at our disposal computers; information storage, analysis, and retrieval systems; networks; exhaustive banks of data on all kinds of subjects; communication satellites; and rapidly evolving and ever-changing television and telephone systems. Though we are inundated with information, many are drowning in ignorance. Indeed, even within the context of this great secular revolution, a key issue is how we translate information into knowledge—how we fit the bits and pieces, the data, into such patterns that we can actually say that we know something. Once having integrated information into knowledge, how do we know that *what* we know is accurate or complete? Scientists and philosophers alike agree that, in a fundamental sense, we don't. All empirical knowledge is provisional, subject to further discoveries and different interpretive models.

Sometimes, however, we confuse our provisional knowledge with the things known. A recent headline in the *New York Times* read: "Mass Found in Elusive Particle; Universe May Never Be the Same."[16] The article suggested that now that scientists know that neutrinos have mass, this will slow the expansion of the universe. Somehow I think the universe is the same today as it was the day before the scientific community revised its theories!

It is possible, therefore, to know without knowing. In fact, it is written that in his dealings with Adam and Eve in the Garden of Eden, Satan, who certainly had lots of information, "knew not the mind of God, wherefore he sought to destroy the world" (Moses 4:6). Paul spoke of those who are "ever learning, and never able to come to the knowledge of the truth" (2 Timothy 3:7). Amos predicted that in our day there would be a famine of "hearing the word of the Lord" (Amos 8:11), and Moroni warned of a latter-day "veil of unbelief" that would keep people in an "awful state of wickedness, and hardness of heart, and blindness of mind" (Ether 4:15).

On the other hand, the Lord has commanded that we serve him with all our minds (D&C 4:2) and that we seek learning by study and by faith (D&C 88:118). He has counseled us to search after knowledge of countries and of kingdoms, of history and of nature, of things past, of things present, and of things to come (D&C 88:79; 93:24, 53). He has promised that the veil will be taken from our minds (D&C 110:1) and that our minds will be enlightened by the Spirit (D&C 11:13). The promise attached to the Word of Wisdom is that the obedient will "find wisdom and great treasures of knowledge, even hidden treasures" (D&C 89:19). As a consequence, we shall be both free and holy (Helaman 14:30; D&C 88:67–68). We shall know the truth, and the truth will make us free (John 8:32).

Free from what? Free from ignorance, sin, and the pangs of death. "If thou shalt ask, thou shalt receive revelation upon revelation, knowledge upon knowledge, that thou mayest know the mysteries and peaceable things—that which bringeth joy, that which bringeth life eternal" (D&C 42:61).

THE CHARACTER OF SPIRITUAL KNOWLEDGE— THE DIVINE PARADIGM

In every field of human intelligence, almost every proposition can be subjected to the question "Why?" Every parent understands this. But, after a lengthy regression of "whys," you reach a point where the only answer is, "Well, that's just the way it is!" In effect, we are saying that is just the way the world is put together. We also know that at times even these "basic truths" are overthrown by additional evidence. Such are the revolutions in the history of science. Is there anything that can be finally established without awaiting further experience? Yes.

There are in this life certain fundamental truths that must be established so firmly in our minds and hearts that no further proof of their veracity is required. To help mortal beings get through the chaos of our existence, our Heavenly Father has provided a certain witness of those crucial understandings within which we can fit the additional light and knowledge we may later receive. We may not know all the answers; indeed, we may not even comprehend all the questions—but revealed truth allows us to establish in our lives a certain framework of understanding that will provide, not only an unshakeable intellectual and spiritual foundation, but transform our very lives.

What is this witness that gives us understanding that transcends the understanding of the senses? It is the witness of the Holy Ghost. The understanding received from the Holy Ghost has three key aspects:

1. It concerns the most critical and transcendent truths

2. It is definitive in its certitude

3. Once received, it changes behavior

Critical and Transcendent Truths

The understanding borne of the witness of the Holy Ghost provides, in the first place, an *architecture of knowledge*—rooms within which additional knowledge can be fit. Another way to put it is that the Holy Ghost provides us with an understanding of the first premises of wisdom. You recall that the Proverbist declared that "the fear of the Lord is the beginning of wisdom: and the knowledge of the holy is understanding" (Proverbs 9:10).

The Prophet Joseph Smith said that there were three certitudes necessary for a man or woman to endure the trials of life: knowledge that God is; an understanding of His nature, attributes, and perfections; and a conviction that the course of life we are pursuing is in accord with His will.[17]

As a student in college, I learned that the original premise or proposition of a syllogism or train of logic is critical. One may work through marvelously sophisticated and complex lines of reasoning, which seem compelling enough at each step; but, if the premise is flawed or incomplete, the whole line of reasoning will also be flawed, no matter how logical or brilliant the deductions.

For instance, if we begin with the premise that life arose by chance and that its development is largely random, we will interpret physical, biological, and social information or data in a certain way. Such a premise will determine how our society operates and how we act. If, on the other hand, we begin with the premise that mortal life arose by design and will develop according to eternal law, we will understand the bits and pieces of our information in an entirely different way—we will see the interconnectedness and wholeness of life. We will grasp the hierarchy of truth, we will see patterns and purpose where others see disorder and chance. Job understood the importance of beginning at a correct premise when searching for truth. Out of the depths of his personal misery, he asked: "But where shall wisdom be found? and where is the place of understanding?" The tormented man explored and dismissed the possibility that wisdom and understanding were to be found in the learning of man or worldly pursuits, then concluded that "the fear of the Lord, *that is wisdom;* and *to depart from evil is understanding* (Job 28:12, 28; emphasis added).

That humans can reason at all is impressive and the result of a divine inheritance each of us receives at birth—the Light of Christ, which "lighteth every man that cometh into the world" (John 1:9). But let us not underestimate the narrowing of perspective that arises from pursuing truth apart from God. I am increasingly struck by the limits and dangers of what Paul would call "carnal" psychology, sociology, philosophy, political science, literature, drama, music, physics, chemistry, and biology.

We must not be limited by theoretical constructs or trapped by scientific explanations that prevent us from "overstepping the limits of time."[18] In this example, we must reject the worldly premise of random and purposeless causality that impels us to ask the wrong questions, focus on the transitory at the expense of the enduring, make improper inferences, and reach incomplete or inaccurate conclusions. In sum, by beginning at an incorrect premise, we risk preaching the transitory doctrines of men instead of established divine truth. If we embrace inaccurate worldly teachings, we risk having a distorted view of things. Or as Paul described it, "we see through a glass darkly," whereas we are invited by God to see Him (and His truths) "face to face." Put another way, Paul said: "My knowledge now is partial, then [when illuminated by the revelation of the Holy Spirit] it will be whole, like God's knowledge of me" (1 Corinthians 13:12, NEB).

All of this explains why the prophets have counseled us to

plumb the depths of the scriptures and the words of the living prophets in faith and prayer. In very deed, the scriptures, under the guidance of the Holy Ghost, constitute the true "guide to the perplexed."[19]

Certitude

Second, as already suggested, worldly knowledge is *definitive.* Although our experiences, observations, and rational faculties may lead us to certain conclusions, empirical data can never compel the kind of conviction that totally dispels doubt and motivates untiring endurance. Jesus told Peter that "flesh and blood" had not led the apostle to know that "Jesus [is] the Christ, the Son of the living God" but rather His "Father which is in heaven" (Matthew 16:17). As Paul wrote, "No man can say that Jesus is the Lord, but by the Holy Ghost" (1 Corinthians 12:3). This explains why it is such a fearful thing to deny the witness of the Holy Ghost. Unlike other evidence, a witness imprinted on us by the Holy Spirit ends any argument. Such verification by the Holy Ghost provides certitude unknown in any other area of thought. There may be many philosophical demonstrations relative to the existence of God or the divine Sonship of Jesus or the truthfulness of the Restoration, but they remain in the arena of speculation, no matter how convincing.

Having a Testimony Changes Our Behavior

Once one has sought and received the witness of the Holy Ghost, one assumes a life-changing obligation. This suggests the third characteristic of this understanding of the Spirit. It is *transforming.* Paul wrote that he had "the mind of Christ" (2 Corinthians 2:16), and having been converted, the people of King

Benjamin declared, "We have no more disposition to do evil but to do good continually" (Mosiah 5:2). They had learned the truth through revelation, and the experience forever altered their focus and behavior. Knowing Christ through the Spirit, we love Him and keep His commandments—and we are further comforted and taught by the Spirit, until we shall be, as Mormon taught, "like him, for we shall see him as he is; that we may have this hope; that we may be purified even as he is pure" (Moroni 7:48; see also 1 John 3:1–3).

In his epistle to the Romans, the Apostle Paul wrote: "And be not conformed to this world: but be ye transformed by the renewing of your mind, that ye may prove what is that good, and acceptable, and perfect, will of God" (Romans 12:2).

Paul distinguishes between a human nature shaped by disobedience and false beliefs and one subject to God and renewed by the Holy Spirit. Only when this renewal begins to take place do we even know the right questions to ask or for what we should correctly pray (see Romans 8:6–8, 26–27). As the Spirit works in us, we receive a "readiness of mind" and are prepared to receive truth and discern "the mind of Christ" (Acts 17:11; 1 Corinthians 2:14, 16).

Alma teaches that as we submit our will to the Father's through faith in Christ, our understanding "doth begin to be enlightened and [our] mind doth begin to expand" (Alma 32:34). In latter days the Lord has said that in order to prosper His people, he "requireth the heart and a willing mind" (D&C 64:34) and has counseled us to "treasure up in [our] minds continually the words of life" (D&C 84:85), sanctifying ourselves that our "minds become single to God, and the day will come that [we] shall see him; for he will unveil his face unto [us]" (D&C 88:68).

The transforming power of spiritual knowledge is not limited to the individual. As Paul observed, as we as a people bend our will to God and make our minds single to His, the community of the Saints will be made perfect, so that there will be no division among us and we will be "perfectly joined together in the same mind and in the same judgment" (1 Corinthians 1:10; see also Romans 14:1, 5, 19).

The Requirements for Obtaining Spiritual Knowledge

How do we attain to such comprehensive, definitive, and transforming knowledge? Let us consider four requirements for obtaining spiritual knowledge:

1. An urgent search for the truth
2. A willingness to obey the truth so discovered
3. A disposition to bear witness to the truth in all places and at all times and
4. A motivation to serve others in truth

Receptivity and Diligent Learning— A Form of Humility

First, then, we must be open to teaching and diligent in our pursuit of the learning of the Spirit. Such a pursuit requires a sense of our own need and more than a casual interest in the answers we seek. The Lord has declared that those who "hunger" and "thirst" after righteousness shall be filled with the Holy Ghost (Matthew 5:6; 3 Nephi 12:6), using the metaphor of physical need to describe our sincerity. But he also warned those who failed to seek spiritual nourishment by declaring, "Woe unto you that are full! For ye shall hunger" (Luke 6:25). The Lord spoke out against those who think themselves self-sufficient or who are indifferent to things of the Spirit, declaring to John the Revelator: "So then because thou art lukewarm, and neither cold nor hot, I will spue thee out of my mouth" (Revelation 3:16–17).

There is a story that a young man once came to Socrates, the ancient Greek philosopher, asking to be taught wisdom. It is reported that Socrates immediately grabbed the young man and thrust his head into an adjacent brook and held it under water. When he finally let him up, gasping for breath, Socrates told him, "When you want wisdom as badly as you wanted air, then I can teach you."[20]

In the poem "Neither out Far Nor in Deep" by Robert Frost, we must be far out and deep into the water of our commitments if anything lasting is to be achieved.[21] The Prophet Joseph Smith attached the search for true understanding to sacrifice and counseled that one can know *the* truth only if one is prepared to sacrifice all things.[22]

The prophets have described those who do not hunger and thirst after righteousness but who are instead indifferent to the teachings of God as having a *"hardness of heart"*—an inability to see what really is, to hear what is truly being said, or to respond with feelings to the promptings of the Spirit. In his final volume of the Narnia tales, *The Last Battle,* C. S. Lewis recounts how, after the forces of the White Witch had been defeated by Aslan the Lion (the Lion representing Christ) and his followers, the prisons and chains with which she had bound so many disappeared. Within a prison stable, a group of dwarves had been chained in a circle. Suddenly, the stable and their chains were gone, and they were free. But they refused to believe their own liberation and stayed within their closed circle, not feeling the fresh air, nor seeing the sun, nor smelling the flowers. Even as Aslan roared in their ears to arouse them, they mistook the roar for thunder or a trick.

As Aslan observed, they had become so afraid of being taken in that they could not be taken out of the prison that was now of their own mind.[23] Aslan observed on another occasion, "Oh, Adam's sons, how cleverly you defend yourself against all that might do you good."[24] In that same spirit, Nephi plaintively wrote, "And now I, Nephi, . . . am left to mourn because of the unbelief, and the wickedness, and the ignorance, and the stiff-neckedness of men; for they will not search knowledge, nor understand great knowledge, when it is given unto them in plainness, even as plain as word can be" (2 Nephi 32:7).

Many cannot hear the whisperings of the Spirit or find the truth because of their insistence on explaining away the miraculous events they are blessed to observe. Many students of Christ seek to explain Him by explaining away His divine Sonship, just as others seek to explain the teachings and revelations of Joseph Smith by dismissing his prophetic calling. As Jacob so wisely observed, it is foolish to repose too much confidence in our limited capacities to observe and understand while rejecting wisdom that comes from the Holy Ghost. But, he concludes, "to be learned is *good if* [we] hearken unto the counsels of God" (2 Nephi 9:28–29; emphasis added).

To be taught wisdom by the Spirit, we must be prepared to invest everything we are. Alma reported that he had "fasted and prayed many days that I might know these things of myself" (Alma 5:46). It requires, then, not only diligent and prayerful study but also the sacrifice of things that may be precious to us, even our own sins, and those elements of our lifestyle that impede learning. We must be willing, as was Lamoni's father, to "give away all [our] sins to know [God]" (Alma 22:18). Jacob's last words summarize the whole matter: "O be wise; what can I say more?" (Jacob 6:12).

Obedience

Having diligently pursued the truth, we must then be prepared to obey the truth. Alma speaks of awakening and arousing our faculties (that is, our hearts and minds) so as to *experiment* upon the word (see Alma 32:27). Surely this refers not to passive learning but active doing. The Apostle John said this of those who say that they know Christ but who fail to follow His counsel, "He that saith, I know him, and keepeth not his commandments, is a liar, and the truth is not in him" (1 John 2:4). The Lord declared as much in the latter days: "And no man receiveth a fulness [of truth] unless he keepeth [God's] commandments. He that keepeth his commandments receiveth truth and light, until he is glorified in truth and knoweth all things" (D&C 93:27–28).

Such seeking and following may also require patience, waiting upon the Lord, who said, "Behold, ye are little children and ye cannot bear all things now; ye must grow in grace and in the knowledge of the truth" (D&C 50:40). And as Elder Neal A. Maxwell has observed, "Striking a balance between seeking and being content to wait for further light and knowledge would appear to be no small task!"[25]

The importance of diligently seeking, learning, and following, accompanied by patient waiting, was well expressed in the words of John Henry Newman—"Keep thou my feet; I do not ask to see the distant scene—one step enough for me."[26] As we follow the truth in obedience, the channels of truth open ever wider to our view, and our lives come to reflect the truth. There is profound meaning in Christ's utterance, "I am the way, the *truth,* and the light" (John 14:6; emphasis added) coupled with his summons to become even as He is (see 3 Nephi 27:27).

Witnessing and Serving

Finally, if we are to acquire spiritual knowledge, we must be prepared to witness the truth we have attained and be willing to serve and edify others in the truth, having, as Enos, "a desire for the welfare of [our] brethren" (Enos 1:9).

In his invitation to the people of King Noah to be baptized, Alma the Elder held up a marvelous standard for those who enter into such a covenant. Those who come to an understanding of the truth and are baptized will have a desire to and will agree to "bear one another's burdens, that they may be light" and to "mourn with those who mourn; yea, and comfort those that stand in need of comfort." Additionally, the believers will be willing to "stand as witnesses of God at all times and in all things, and in all places" (Mosiah 18:8–9). And, having come to this new understanding and way of life, another promise is realized: "Then shall thy confidence wax strong in the presence of God; and the doctrine of the priesthood shall distill upon thy soul as the dews from heaven. The Holy Ghost shall be thy constant companion" (D&C 121:45–46).

Sanctified by this change in our knowledge and behavior, we also attain a certitude that banishes doubt and fear and, with Nephi and Paul, are able to confront the challenges of life with the "perfect brightness of hope" (2 Nephi 31:20) that nothing "shall be able to separate us from the love of God, which is in Christ Jesus our Lord" (Romans 8:39).

CHAPTER 2

Adapt Yourselves No Longer to the Pattern of This Present World

During a season of great spiritual insight in Kirtland, Ohio, one of the remarkable revelations that was received was the declaration of Christ concerning both His and our nature and our relationship to each other and to the Father. This declaration, which was to become Section 93 of the Doctrine and Covenants, declared that Christ was in the beginning with the Father and was the Firstborn. Moreover, mankind was also in the beginning with the Father. The revelation then reads, "For man is spirit" (D&C 93:33). This statement and its explication in the revelation point to the destiny of all men and women, their duties, and the requirements for their happiness. Taking this revelation as our text, let us consider the dimensions of spirituality and, conversely, the conditions of spiritual death.

FALLEN MAN

Let me draw your attention to a comic-strip character with whom I believe many of you may be acquainted. He is lazy, selfish, inconsiderate, boorish, and disloyal—all those traits with which we can at times identify! His name is Andy Capp.

> ANDY (behind girl): Whistles, but as he passes the church, he puts a coin in the contribution box.
> PARSON (standing in the doorway of the church): "Thanks, Andy. You'll go to heaven."
> ANDY: Continues after girl.
> PARSON (looking after him, thinks): *But I don't think you'll like it.*

On another occasion—

> ANDY (coming in the door looking downcast): "Let's face it Flo—I'm just a miserable sinner."
> FLO: "Poppycock!" (looks out from comic strip) "—E's the happiest little sinner I've ever come across."

Is one to deduce from this that sin is fun? In a sense, yes. While sin is a miserable condition likened unto death, the problem of sin is that we indeed desire—and in a sense enjoy—evil, even to the extent that we cannot appreciate or feel entirely comfortable with good. C. S. Lewis once observed that heaven is for those who want it; hell is for those who desire it.[27] We do in fact get what we desire. More, we *become* what we desire. If we desire evil pleasures, we will likely shun the pleasures of heaven, and in the process, become ourselves perdition. There is a universal application to Christ's teaching that "He that seeketh findeth" (Luke 11:10).

If we seek pleasures less than those of the celestial kingdom, we shall most certainly have them. For of those who pursue such things, the Master said, "They have their reward" (Matthew 6:16).

They get—and grow into the image of—what they desire. The Book of Mormon refers to this process as the principle of restoration. As Alma described it:

> It is requisite with the justice of God that men should be judged according to their works; and if their works were good in this life, and the desires of their hearts were good, that they should also, at the last day, be restored unto that which is good. And if their works are evil they shall be restored unto them for evil. . . . The one raised to happiness according to his desires of happiness, or good according to his desires of good; and the other to evil according to his desires of evil; for as he has desired to do evil all the day long even so shall he have his reward of evil when the night cometh. . . . For behold, they are their own judges, whether to do good or do evil. [Alma 41:3, 4, 5, 7.]

Andy Capp's rent collector may have grasped how one gets and becomes what one desires. One day as Andy is leaving home, Flo says to him, "'Ave a nice time, pet, an' try not to get into bad company." The rent collector, overhearing this charge, thinks to himself, *She's got to be kiddin'—that bloke's in bad company when 'es on 'is own!*

It was Milton's Satan in *Paradise Lost* who exclaimed,

> *Myself am Hell;*
> *And in the lowest deep,*
> *a lower deep,*
> *Still threat'ning to devour me,*
> *opens wide;*

46

To which the hell I suffer seems
a heaven.[28]

This condition is called in the scriptures "spiritual death." It is man in a "fallen" condition. As Alma explained,

Our first parents were cut off both temporally and spiritually from the presence of the Lord . . . Therefore, as the soul could never die, and the fall had brought upon all mankind a spiritual death as well as a temporal, that is, they were cut off from the presence of the Lord, it was expedient that mankind should be reclaimed from this spiritual death . . . [for] they had become carnal, sensual, and devilish, by nature. [Alma 42:7–11]

Note men in the fallen condition don't simply *do* carnal, sensual, and devilish things, but they become such "by nature." Spiritual death, the fallen condition, thus includes not only evil acts but also faulty understanding, corrupt feelings, and base aspirations, as well as ignoble actions.

Faulty Understanding

Let me signal two aspects of the faulty understanding accompanying spiritual death: Faulty perceptions and faulty intellect.

Faulty Perceptions

Christ taught that there is a critical connection between believing and seeing. If seeing is believing, so, more fundamentally, believing is the basis of seeing—"He that believeth on the Son hath everlasting life: and he that believeth not the Son shall not *see* life. . . . In him was life; and the life was the light of men" (John 3:36; 1:4; emphasis added).

J. P. Jacks, a professor at Manchester College, Oxford, used to play a game with his guests where he would ask them to scan his parlor and fix in their minds all the items they could see. After they had all spent a minute or two observing the room, they would be invited into an adjoining room where they were to list on paper all the items they could remember. They would then return to the parlor and compare their lists to see how thorough-going they were in their observations. While they were doing so, Professor Jacks would go over to the light switch by the door and turn off the light. Suddenly the room would go black, demonstrating to the guests the one thing they almost always failed to observe—the light whereby everything was perceived and put into perspective.[29] The point is clear: often we go through life, failing to see the light wherein we live and have our being.

Similarly, in days past when I taught undergraduates, I would often divide the class in half, separated by an aisle. Without one side of the class seeing what I would show the other, I had each study a picture of a woman, but they were different pictures for each half. On the left, the picture was of an old, rather dowdy woman with large features; on the right the picture was of a chic young woman with delicate features. Having let the students fix in their minds for a period of minutes the image they were seeing, I would remove the pictures and flash on a screen at the front of the classroom a composite picture, one in which the two pictures were melded together. I then asked the class what they were seeing, and they all agreed it was a woman. This was the last accord they had. After that, each side of the class described what they had been conditioned to see: those on my left described an old woman; those on my right a young woman; those on the left a dowdy woman with large features; those on the right a chic young woman with delicate features. I would then trace with my finger on the screen the separate outlines of the two women. What is interesting is that even with my help, about 30 percent of the class still could not see that there was a second image in the picture—and many were never able to pick out the alternative visage. Now this is a psycho-physical phenomenon, I know, but I wonder whether there aren't spiritual analogies. Having eyes to see and seeing not, ears to hear and hearing not, hearts to feel and feeling not—no defects can be so deadly, dead "as to things pertaining unto righteousness."

Faulty Intellect

The Apostle Paul described those persons who are "ever learning, and never able to come to the knowledge of the truth" (2 Timothy 3:7). As Elder Neal A. Maxwell so astutely observed: "So much of the secular data men have accumulated is accurate, but ultimately unimportant. Even learning useful things has often diverted mankind from learning crucial things."[30]

In the Book of Mormon, Jacob addresses this issue of faulty intellect, a worldly wisdom that is but foolishness—

> O that cunning plan of the evil one! O the vainness, and the frailties, and the foolishness of men! When they are learned they think they are wise, and they hearken not unto the counsel of God, for they set it aside, supposing they know of themselves, wherefore, their wisdom is foolishness and it profiteth them not. And they shall perish. [2 Nephi 9:28]

Few things are as important in life as getting the questions right—and thus being able to appreciate the scope of our ignorance. Socrates argued that, as to many of the great questions of life, he did not know the answers. But, as he said, he was better off than all the others around him who also didn't know, but did not know that they did not know.[31]

Unless we become aware of the defining questions of our existence, we can never appreciate the limits of our understanding and thus cannot be taught. One could argue that the reason our society is so frustrated with the answers that are being given to our collective problems is that we have failed to pose the proper questions.

The Jewish teacher Abraham Heschel argued that the reason that the counsel of holy scriptures has been so marginalized in much of our society is that they raise questions that we are no longer asking. As he observed:

> The most serious obstacle which modern men encounter in entering a discussion about the ideas of the Bible, is the absence from man's consciousness of the problem to which the Bible refers. This, indeed, is the status of the Bible in modern society: it is a sublime answer, but we no longer know the question to which it responds. Unless we recover the question, there is no hope of understanding the Bible.
>
> The Bible is an answer to the question, what does God require of man? But to modern man, this question is suppressed by another one, namely, what does man demand of God? Modern man continues to ponder: what will I get out of life? What escapes his attention is the fundamental question, what will life get out of me?[32]

CORRUPT FEELINGS

If faulty understanding, with its accompanying defects of perspective and intellect, is one of the fruits of man's fallen condition, so, too, corrupt feelings are another characteristic of spiritual death. Nephi pointed out to his rebellious brothers that even though they had seen an angel and been rebuked by him and had had other spiritual manifestations, they were incapable of changing their behavior, saying, "ye were past feeling, that ye could not feel his words" (1 Nephi 17:45). The scriptures often refer to feelings in terms of the heart and an inability to pay heed to spiritual things as a "hardness of heart."

In such a state, as John noted, "men love darkness rather than light" (John 3:19). President David O. McKay, ninth President of the Church, once observed that though may we be surrounded by myriad voices and sounds, we hear them according to whether or not our soul is tuned to the same key. And, if the soul be defective in its tuning, it will respond to corrupt voices and interpret noise as music, whereas it will be unable to hear the voice of God and the music of His created world. As President McKay said, "If then, the soul be tuned to the same key [as that of God] so as to give a true response, rest assured that our lives will be filled with harmony and joy, for God's hand never strikes a discord."[33]

Feelings of anger, rage, lust, greed, and so forth are often seen as "natural," and we are told that it is not in our feelings that we sin, but in our behavior. The key to proper living, in this view, is thus to control the external expression of our inner feelings. Note, however, that the prophets have all declared that, in fact, we may sin in our feelings. Paul wrote, "Can ye be angry, and not sin?" (JST Ephesians 4:26). The apostle then counseled the Ephesians, "Let all bitterness, and wrath, and anger, and clamor, and evil speaking, be put away from you, with all malice, and be ye kind one to another, tenderhearted, forgiving one another, even as God for Christ's sake hath forgiven you" (Ephesians 4:31–32). Moreover, in the Sermon on the Mount, Christ centered sin in our sentiments, the imaginations of our heart, rather than simply in our acts (see Matthew 5). Indeed, Jesus condemned even thinking evil in our hearts (see Matthew 9:4) and commended the "pure in heart," who he said "shall see God" (Matthew 5:8). King Benjamin taught that if we walk in the Light of Christ, we will "have no more disposition to do evil, but to do good continually" (Mosiah 5:2).

BASE ASPIRATIONS

Closely associated with faulty understanding and corrupt feelings are base aspirations. Base aspirations include not only ignoble goals but excessively small plans, inappropriate priorities, and desired ends that are wide of the mark of our eternal potential.

As I was finishing up my graduate work, I had to decide exactly what I would do and where I would work. I had several possibilities to choose from and was uncertain which course I should pursue. I prayed to my Father in Heaven, asking him which of the courses before me I should follow. And, as often happens, no inspiration seemed to come. But this, I felt, was too important a question to accept silence. So I prayed and fasted as I seldom have.

The problem with praying with sincerity and real intent is that divine counsel may indeed come—but it may not be what one expects or welcomes. Indeed, when the Lord speaks, it often requires a change of life or a different set of questions. This is why the missionaries seek to have those they are teaching to pray—and why those being taught often resist this invitation. Investigators seem to understand that, if they pose the question as to the truthfulness of the gospel, they may have to alter their lives. It is a bit like the saying, "If you can't abide by the answer, don't ask the question!"

But so it was with me. The answer did come as clearly as any inspiration I ever received and it was startling. For it was, "It doesn't matter." This was not what I expected! How could my Heavenly Father not care whether I stay in Massachusetts, or go to Virginia, or take this job or that? But the rest of the answer made this clear: "It is not where you go or what you shall do in your career that is fundamentally important. I expect you to pursue your profession diligently and honorably and make the best contribution you can. But far more important than where you are or what work you pursue is whether or not you shall keep my commandments, bless your family, and strive to build my kingdom and establish the cause of Zion." The Lord was seeking to change, if not the questions I was asking, the way in which I was posing them. He was seeking to ensure that I did not lose sight of my eternal goal and its divine priorities. Much unhappiness in this life results from aspiring to less than what we can be and by failing to vigorously pursue the revealed purposes of life.

IGNOBLE ACTIONS

Finally, fallen men and women act out the imaginations of their hearts. If Christ was the *Logos,* the mortal expression of God's purposes and being, so each of us expresses in our mortal acts the essence and character of our inner beings. The wickedness we see around us is not random acts but the expression of profound social and personal corruption—of a spiritual death that grips the very heart and mind.

What is perhaps most ironical about this fallen state is that those who have descended therein wish to be happy—and indeed often feel themselves thus. Whether it be because of the corrupt traditions of their parents or because of simple inertia or because of conscious disobedience to the commands of God, those who become alienated from the divine order believe they seek life, not death (see D&C 93:38–39). Mormon, reflecting on the fate of Korihor the anti-Christ, made the melancholy observation: "And thus we see that the devil will not support his children . . . but doth speedily drag them down to hell" (Alma 30:60).

An odd sort of pleasure are the attractions of hell. Those so attracted often seem to glory in their sins—and the associated miseries. They would rather itch in order to scratch, to have a hangover for what C. S. Lewis describes as "the delicious sense of feeling sorry for oneself." The senior devil in *The Screwtape Letters* described the pleasure formula of hell: "An ever increasing craving for an ever diminishing pleasure."[34] Some years ago in an unusual burst of candor, a cigarette company in one of their advertisements asked, "Are you smoking more now but enjoying it less?" And so it is with such pleasures.

Again, we do get what we desire, but what we desire being so out of harmony with our divine potential, we feel the coldness of death even in the midst of life—and find that life eternal eludes us even after death. We develop cravings which, rather than being fulfilled, remain unsatisfied—and indeed grow throughout eternity. Hell indeed! As Samuel the prophet said to the wayward Nephites: "Ye have sought all the days of your lives for that which ye could not obtain; and ye have sought for happiness in doing iniquity, which thing is contrary to the nature of that righteousness which is in our great and Eternal Head" (Helaman 13:38).

Alma described this spiritual death as being—

> . . . without God in the world . . . gone contrary to the nature of God . . . in a state contrary to the nature of happiness . . . knowing evil from good [but] subjecting themselves to the devil . . . in the ways of sin and rebellion against God . . . an enemy to God . . . gone according to their own carnal wills and desires; having never called upon the Lord while the arms of mercy were extended towards them. [Alma 41:11; Mosiah 16:3, 5, 12]

In this state, Alma describes such fallen individuals as "consigned . . . forever to be cut off from [God's] presence" (Alma 42:14). What an infinite corruption is this—and what an infinite atonement and unqualified faith and repentance it would take to overcome.

One day Lucy is talking to Charlie Brown and says, "Sooner or later, Charlie Brown, there's one thing you're going to have to learn . . . you reap what you sow; you get out of life exactly what you put into it. No more and no less." Snoopy, overhearing this conversation, thinks to himself, *I'd kind of like to see a little more margin for error.*

Even Lucy herself apparently has similar desires. One day she is yelling at her mother in the next room: "I'm my own woman! I'm strong and capable! I can do it my way!" And then she says almost inaudibly, " . . . with a little help."

King Benjamin clearly described the condition of fallen man when he addressed his people. He testified of the critical help needed to redeem mankind from this awful state—and pointed to the nature and conditions of spirituality. As he said:

For the natural man is an enemy to God, and has been from the fall of Adam, and will be, forever and ever, unless he yields to the enticings of the Holy Spirit, and putteth off the natural man and becometh a saint through the atonement of Christ the Lord, and becometh as a child, submissive, meek, humble, patient, full of love, willing to submit to all things which the Lord seeth fit to inflict upon him, even as a child doth submit to his father. [Mosiah 3:19]

THINGS OF THE SPIRIT

If we are to hear, see, and feel the things of the Spirit, we must yield to the promise and the requirements of the Atonement. We must, as if children, begin to discern as if for the first time.

As part of a meeting of the leadership of the North America Northeast Area of the Church, I was able to attend an historic assembly on 6 November 1993. For the first time since the Saints left Kirtland in the late 1830s, authorized priesthood leaders were able to conduct a sacrament meeting in the Kirtland Temple. In attendance were Elder M. Russell Ballard of the Council of the Twelve Apostles and Elders Cree-L Kofford, Yoshihiko Kikuchi, Joe J. Christensen, and Marlin K. Jensen, all of the Seventy.

Elder Ballard and Elder Kofford blessed the sacrament. In doing so, they knelt immediately beneath the breastwork of the pulpit where Jesus Christ, followed by Moses, Elias, and Elijah, appeared to Joseph Smith and Oliver Cowdery on the day of Passover, 3 April 1836. Then they and the other General Authorities passed the tokens of the Lord's Supper to the assembly. As extraordinary as the place where the sacrament was being blessed, was the fact that one of the men blessing the sacrament was Elder Ballard, a direct descendent of Hyrum Smith, the last individual to have administered the sacrament prior to the Saints' withdrawal from Kirtland. Moreover, Elder Kofford was himself a direct descendent of one who supervised the masonry work on the temple.

As soon as all of those present had assembled for the meeting, the very air was charged with the Holy Spirit. Tears welled up in every eye, hearts began to burn, the distant strains of the temple anthem, "The Spirit of God like a fire is burning," seemed to ring in every ear, and one could almost hear the testimony of Joseph and Oliver and the words uttered by the risen Savior:

> The veil was taken from our minds, and the eyes of our understanding were opened. We saw the Lord standing upon the breastwork of the pulpit, before us; . . . [saying] I am the first and the last; I am he who liveth, I am he who was slain; I am your advocate with the Father. Behold, your sins are forgiven you; you are clean before me; therefore, lift up your voice and rejoice. [D&C 110:1, 3–5]

Elder Kikuchi, who first heard the gospel in a land far distant from Kirtland, trembled with emotion as he recalled what the Lord declared on that April day:

> Yea the hearts of thousands and tens of thousands shall greatly rejoice in consequences of the blessings which shall be poured out. . . . And the fame of this house shall spread to foreign lands; and this is the beginning of the blessing which shall be poured out upon the heads of my people. [D&C 110:9–10]

Looked at coldly, this assembly was but an ordinary sacrament meeting: prayers were given, songs sung, remarks made, and the sacrament blessed. To an outsider, that is all that it might have appeared to be. But not for those of us who were there assembled. We had eyes that saw, ears that heard, and bosoms that burned in ways that are difficult to communicate. It was not the externals of the event that were important but the connection of Spirit to spirit.

It is recorded in the gospel of John that after Jesus' triumphant entry into Jerusalem on the eve of the Passover and shortly before His crucifixion, He, in the presence of the multitude, declared: "The hour is come, that the Son of man should be glorified. . . . Then came there a voice from heaven, saying, I have both glorified [the Father's name], and will glorify it again" (John 12:23, 28).

And what did the assembled crowd hear and see? Some heard what they thought was thunder, others said an angel had spoken, but few discerned the voice of God. Some were confused and inquired of Jesus, "We have heard out of the law that Christ abideth for ever: and how sayest thou, The Son of man must be lifted up? who is this Son of man?" (John 12:34). Noting that few had understood His identity and mission, Christ reminded the people that though He had done many miracles among them, yet they believed not on Him. He cited Isaiah, who had prophesied the disbelief of the people (Isaiah 53:1), and He indicated that Satan had "blinded their eyes, and hardened their heart; that they should not see with their eyes, nor understand with their heart, and be converted" (John 12: 40).

He called His disciples to walk in the light:

Walk while ye have the light, lest darkness come upon you: for he that walketh in darkness knoweth not whither

he goeth. While ye have the light, believe in the light, that
ye may be the children of light. . . . I am come a light into
the world, that whosoever believeth on me should not
abide in darkness. [John 12:35–36, 46]

The Savior also pointed to a key reward of spiritual discern-
ment: "And he that seeth me seeth him that sent me" (John
12:45).

DEFINITION OF SPIRITUALITY

What, then, is spirituality—and what is it not?

Spirituality is *not* essentially a sensation or momentary inspiration but a state of being—who we are and who we are
becoming.

• Spirituality should not be confused with experiences,
although spirituality will cause us to discern within experiences
things hitherto unseen, unheard, and unfelt.

• Spirituality should not be confused with zealous enthusiasm
or a pious demeanor, although spirituality will lead to divine optimism and genuine reverence.

• Spirituality should not be seen as ultimately determined by
external circumstances, although all such circumstances carry
within them consequences for our eternal being.

All things that happen in mortal time have spiritual roots and
consequences; that is, they reveal patterns of existence and can
reinforce or detract from our eternal destiny. The Lord indicates
in the 88th section of the Doctrine and Covenants that in this
mortal life there are already revealed celestial, terrestrial, and teles-
tial orders of glory, as well as domains not of glory. Spirituality
then should not be an interlude or spectacular moment in our life

but the very fabric of our life—a search after the mind and will of God and a willingness to follow that mind and will. Spirituality is not a momentary "high" or an escape from the dilemmas of the world but triumph in the world and beyond the world.

David O. McKay observed—

> Spirituality is the consciousness of victory over self and of communion with the infinite. Spirituality impels one to conquer difficulties and acquire more and more strength. To feel one's faculties unfolding and truth expanding the soul is one of life's sublimest experiences. Being 'honest, true, chaste, benevolent, virtuous, and in doing good to all men' are attributes which contribute to spirituality, the highest acquisition of the soul. It is the divine in man, the supreme crowning gift that makes him king of all created things, the one final quality that makes him tower above all other animals.[35]

DIMENSIONS OF SPIRITUALITY: UNDERSTANDING, FEELINGS, DESIRES, BEHAVIOR

Earlier we discussed the dimensions of fallen men—defects in understanding, feelings, aspirations or desires, and behavior. The dimensions of spirituality necessarily involve the same categories. Let us explore them from the positive rather than the negative side.

Understanding

As the 93rd section of the Doctrine and Covenants makes clear and as Joseph Smith expounded in many sermons, a key aspect of spirituality is understanding: "The glory of God is intelligence, or, in other words, light and truth" (v. 36). It was revealed to the Prophet that he who obeys the commandments "receiveth truth and light, until he is glorified in truth and knoweth all things" (v. 28), and that Christ is "the true light that lighteth every man that cometh into the world" (v. 2). *Intelligence, light, truth*—these are ordinary words used in both ordinary and out-of-the-ordinary ways in this revelation. To grasp their meaning and their import, however, is to understand what Paul described as the "hidden wisdom, which God ordained before the world unto our glory" (1 Corinthians 2:7).

The 93rd section defines truth as "knowledge of things as they are, and as they were, and as they are to come" (v. 24), conformity to which leads to fulfillment, perfection, happiness. In a dictionary sense, *truth* has several meanings and shades of meaning:

- Actual state of affairs
- Fundamental reality transcending perceived experience
- Conformity with fact
- Agreement with a standard or original
- Honesty, integrity

All of these meanings are useful in understanding the statements in the Doctrine and Covenants, but I find the notion of "fundamental reality transcending perceived experience" and "agreement with a standard or original" most helpful.

Light too, is seen as an essential component of intelligence. Again, there are several shades of meaning in the lexicon, all of which may help our understanding of this aspect of intelligence:

- Something that makes things visible
- An illuminating agent
- Spiritual illumination or enlightenment
- A means of igniting, as a spark or flame

A key understanding provided by Doctrine and Covenants 93 is that man is in a fundamental way not the product of *creation* (ex nihilo, as it were) but of *generation*. That is, as Christ is the first begotten spirit child of the Father, so we are also begotten of the Father: He is the Father of our spirits, which spirits are composed of eternally existent material which is simply called "intelligence." We know virtually nothing about this eternal substance, save it "was not created or made, neither indeed can be" (v. 29) and that it carries within it a divine potential and the basis of moral agency (see v. 30). In any case, the Lord has declared, "Man is spirit"; that is, he is a conscious, intelligent, individual entity that had an existence previous to mortality and is literally a spirit son or daughter of Deity—which explains why God is referred to as our *Heavenly* Father.

The 93rd section further declares that the eternal order, the eternal potential within, can only be realized if the spirit is joined inseparably to the body (v. 33) to constitute the mortal soul (see D&C 88:15). Only if spirit and body, or "element," are inseparably connected can man be fulfilled or receive a fullness of joy (v. 34).

Christ Himself is not only the first begotten spirit of the Father, but He is the Only Begotten Son in the flesh. We, also begotten by the Father in the spirit, are begotten in the flesh by mortal fathers and mothers. Jesus' unique nature—begotten in the flesh by an immortal Father and a mortal mother—explains in part why Christ was able to rise from the dead to become the "first fruits of them that slept" (1 Corinthians 15:20), He being the first on this earth to have an eternal spirit and mortal element eternally united. Part of the "good news" of the gospel is that Christ makes the resurrection universally available. The other part is that by virtue of His atonement and upon condition of our faith in Him

unto repentance, He will remove from us the weight and consequences of our own sins. Under the hand of those authorized by
Him, we may be baptized for the remission of our sins and receive
the gift of the Holy Ghost, which not only establishes our repentance and our willingness to live in a covenant relationship with
God, but provides that power of the Holy Ghost, whereby we may
ultimately be sanctified and made perfect.

As we follow Christ and thus pursue the eternal potential that
lies within each of us, He becomes not only our "advocate with
the Father" (D&C 45:3–5) but, in a real sense, *our Father,* "the
author of eternal salvation unto all them that obey him" (Hebrews
5:9). In that poignant scene that has come to be called the Last
Supper, Christ offered this magnificent prayer:

> Neither pray I for these alone, but for them also which
> shall believe on me through their word; That they all may
> be one; as thou, Father, are in me, and I in thee, that they
> also may be one in us: . . . And the glory which thou
> gavest me I have given them; that they may be one, even
> as we are one. [John 17:20–22]

That is, the Father and the Son are unified in what they have
revealed to be their goal: "For behold, this is my work and my
glory—to bring to pass the immortality and eternal life of man"
(Moses 1:39).

Remarkably, they invite us into that divine partnership, to the
end that we may ultimately be like them. Which is why, as John
observed, "when [Christ] shall appear, we shall be like him; for we
shall see him as he is" (1 John 3:2). That work is to ensure the fullness of godliness to God's spiritually begotten sons and daughters,
whose spirits, enlivened by eternal intelligence and embodied in
perfected, incorruptible, resurrected bodies, will live with them

forever. This divine pattern of eternal potential and spiritual generation revealed in Christ is *The* Truth and *The* Light. It is the
glory to which our eye should be single. It is what the Lord was
teaching us when he declared, "The glory of God is intelligence,
or, in other words, light and truth" (D&C 93:36). This is also the
answer to the query of the hymn, "Oh Say, What Is Truth?" As
the words of the hymn read:

> *Then say, what is truth?*
> *'Tis the last and the first,*
> *For the limits of time it steps o'er.*
> *Tho the heavens depart*
> *And the earth's fountains burst,*
> *Truth, the sum of existence,*
> *Will weather the worst,*
> *Eternal, unchanged, evermore.* [36]

It is with this understanding that the Apostle Paul wrote to the
Romans:

> The Spirit you have received is not a spirit of slavery
> leading you back into a life of fear, but a Spirit that makes
> us sons, enabling us to cry "Abba! Father!" In that cry, the
> Spirit of God joins with our spirit in testifying that we are
> God's children; and if children, then heirs. We are God's
> heirs and Christ's fellow-heirs, if we share his suffering
> now in order to share his splendor hereafter. . . . For God
> knew his own before ever they were and also ordained that
> they should be shaped to the likeness of his Son, that he
> might be the eldest among a large family of brothers. . . .
> Adapt yourself no longer to the pattern of this present
> world, but let your minds be remade and your whole

nature thus transformed. Then you will be able to discern the will of God, and to know what is good, acceptable, and perfect. (Romans 6:3–4, 6–8, 16, 19; 8:5–6, 15–17, 29–30; 12:2—NEB)

Feelings

Another measure of our spirituality is our ability to resonate to spiritual feelings. Alma the Younger asked his people if they had "experienced a change of heart, and if [they] had *felt* to sing the song of redeeming love." If so, he asked, "can ye *feel* so now?" (Alma 5:26; emphasis added). The prophet Ezra spoke of *preparing his heart* in order to seek the law of God (see Ezra 7:10), and Solomon counseled that we apply our heart[s] to understanding (see Proverbs 2:2). God, speaking through Ezekiel, told Israel that He would make them "a new heart and a new spirit" (Ezekiel 18:31). And relative to the spirit of revelation, the Lord counseled Oliver Cowdery: "Behold, . . . you must study it out in your mind; then you must ask me if it be right, and if it is right I will cause that your bosom shall burn within you; therefore, you shall *feel* that it is right" (D&C 9:8; emphasis added). Nothing contributes more to our spirituality than thinking ennobling thoughts, having a discerning sensibility, and possessing a heart that is attuned to the mystic chords of a world that shows forth the glory of God. On the other hand, nothing is more destructive of our spirituality than the loss of our ability to discern or *feel* spiritual things. Indeed, it is possible to reach a condition where the Spirit of the Lord ceases to strive with us. It was this awful state that led Mormon to despair for his people, who had so hardened their hearts that they were "without order and without mercy. . . . Without principle and past feeling" (Moroni 9:18, 20).

In latter-days, the Lord speaks of Satan's having a hold on evil men's hearts, a corruption so profound that "they love darkness rather than light" (D&C 10:20–21).

I am increasingly persuaded that men are not led to do evil by logical discourse or reasoned arguments. Satan's strength lies not in the power of his arguments but in his skillful and subtle corruption of our very sentiments. In the world of military strategy, one speaks of *indirect* versus *direct* assault. And the most powerful weapon of the indirect strategy in the moral world is the use of what I would broadly call "poetry."

By poetry, I mean not simply verse or poems, but the use of artistic form, musical rhythms, dramatic expression, rhetorical formulas—in a word, the whole of art as defined today most powerfully in television, movies, and popular music. Plato long ago noted that such "poetry" predisposes the soul either toward wisdom, justice, and mercy or toward folly, prejudice, and viciousness.[37]

In one of the sales catalogues that my wife and I received in the mail, there was an advertisement for a T-shirt upon which had been reproduced one of the garish art works of Fred Babb, upon which he had superimposed the words, "Art can't hurt you." The fact is that art can hurt or it can edify, for one of the characteristics of art is its power to shape our feelings and contribute to the very contours of our soul. The character or intent of the artist is therefore relevant in our assessment of his or her creation and the range and nature of its influence.

I was struck some years ago by the suicide of a person the newspaper described as the "rock icon," Kurt Cobain. As is often the case, his life was described in terms of the drugs and disorientation of the life associated with much contemporary entertainment. In reaction to his suicide, his mother exclaimed, "Now he's gone to join that stupid club," referring to the similar fate of such rock stars as Jim Morrison and Jimi Hendrix. In describing the group, Nirvana, of which Cobain was the lead singer, the reporter wrote, "Nirvana, with its punk-rock spirit, distorted guitars, and alienated lyrics, spearheaded the so-called 'grunge' movement . . . [and] showed an uncanny ability to move from subdued, even pretty passages (some accompanied by cello) to seething sonic rampage." The reporter quoted Cobain as having said, "There's a bunch of people who are concerned with what I have to say. I find that frightening at times, because I'm just as confused as most people."[38]

Indeed, such a thought should be frightening. In the bitter-sweet lyrics of one of Nirvana's releases, the group sings "Teenage angst has paid off well/Now I'm bored and old." The world-weariness, the alienation from the divine, and the celebration of death found in many such lyrics and rhythms threaten to corrupt the feelings and scar the souls of multitudes. Moses invited the children of Israel to choose life over death. And in their warnings against pornography, filth, and debauchery disguised as art, contemporary prophets are making the same plea.

If we are intent on hearing the voice of God in our daily lives, we must be careful to reduce the noise level around us and to eschew the voices of lesser gods that will corrupt us and then abandon us. If we have been led to sing the song of redeeming love and wish to feel that same sentiment now, we need to evaluate whether the influences of the eye and of the ear lean in that direction or not. Perhaps Christ put it most dramatically—and, I take it, metaphorically—when He said that if our eye offends us, we should pluck it out (see Matthew 5:29). In dramatic form He called our attention to those images and forms of expression that may corrupt our very feelings and hence destroy our ability to have the law of God written "not in tables of stone, but in fleshy tables of [our] hearts" (2 Corinthians 3:2). In the hymn "School Thy Feelings," poet Charles W. Penrose reflected insightfully on this truth:

> *Noblest minds have finest feelings . . .*
> *Tune them with the key of love. . . .*
> *Hearts so sensitively molded*
> *Strongly fortified should be,*
> *Trained to firmness and enfolded*
> *In a calm tranquility.*[39]

Desires

President David O. McKay once remarked that few things are as tragic in life as low aim.[40] The intent, the nature, and the focus of our desires are key components of spirituality. The words of another familiar hymn, "Come, Follow Me," capture the high aim that President McKay felt should govern all our plans:

> *"Come, follow me," the Savior said.*
> *Then let us in his footsteps tread,*
> *For thus alone can we be one*
> *With God's own loved, begotten Son. . . .*
>
> *For thrones, dominions, kingdoms, powers,*
> *And glory great and bliss are ours,*
> *If we, throughout eternity,*
> *Obey his words, "Come, follow me."*[41]

The Apostle Paul called upon the former-day Saints to "think big." As he told the Corinthians, he spoke to them not with subtle arguments but with conviction born of spiritual power. For, only

by spirit to spirit could he communicate the glorious consummation that awaited their lives if they would but aim at that purpose
for which they had been created. As he wrote—

> I speak God's hidden wisdom, his secret purpose
> framed from the very beginning to bring us to our full
> glory. The powers that rule the world have never known
> it . . . But, in the words of scripture, "things beyond our
> seeing, things beyond our hearing, things beyond our
> imagining, all prepared by God for those who love him,"
> these it is that God has revealed to us through the Spirit.
> [1 Corinthians 2:7–10, NEB]

Before the present earth was framed, we met in council and
heard the plan that was to guide us to divine fulfillment. Applying
this premortal model, Adam, the patriarch, and the prophets each
made individual plans for themselves, their families, and their
communities, in order to bring to pass the immortality and the
eternal life of man. Christ warned us about planning and building houses upon sand that could not withstand the fierce gales and
the pounding waves (see Luke 6:48).

And yet, many of us get so caught up in what we choose to
call the "daily grind" that we miss the glory that stands revealed
before us. This mortal body, with all its frailties, has empowered
us in ways that Satan and his minions can only envy. The human
body can experience heightened sensibilities; reveal the dimensions of pleasure and pain; deepen our consciousness of all the
hues, the colors, and the contrasts of living; and be the instrument
of procreation, of mortal generation. The challenges and the
opportunities, the ups and the downs of life, are not peripheral
but central to the meaning of our mortal journey. So often, however, we are so focused on the combat raging around our personal

foxhole that we lose sight of the larger battle of which we are a part and of the distant objective for which we entered into the struggle. We live in time, but armed with the truth centered in Christ, we can—we must—step over the limits of time.

Lowell Thomas, the famous world traveler and news commentator, once remarked that, in a figurative sense, many people want to bag an elephant in this life, but they never do what is necessary to achieve that goal. That is, they do not go where elephants are, they are armed only with squirrel guns, and they aim at something which is not an elephant—and then bemoan the fact that they never got their elephant.[42] The problem of life is, even if we have high aspirations, we often neither plan nor act in such a way as to achieve those goals. And most never perceive the connection between the beginning and the end.

In the well-known play *Our Town,* one of the principal characters is a stage manager, who sets the scene for the audience and then discusses with them what is taking place on the stage. In one scene he motions to a couple sitting across a breakfast table from each other. He notes that the man is a lawyer and that she and he have raised a family and eaten a multitude of meals across that table. He then asks, "How do such things begin?" and remarks that "the beginning of all things is frail and weak. Therefore, ever keep your eye on the beginnings."[43]

Having a divine vision and a clearly defined objective translated into a plan of action—these, then, are also key dimensions of spirituality.

Behavior

In the end, all our understanding, our feelings, and our desires are demonstrated in our actions. Once we have received the truth which is in Christ, we will thereby be perfected in truth, and this through obedience to that Truth and that Light—

> The Spirit of truth is of God. I am the Spirit of truth, and John bore record of me, saying: He receiveth a fulness of truth, yea, even of all truth. And no man receiveth a fulness unless he keepeth his commandments. He that keepeth his commandments receiveth truth and light, until he is glorified in truth and knoweth all things. [D&C 93:26–28]

In some interesting passages in the 88th section of the Doctrine and Covenants, the Lord points to typical, perhaps archetypical, aspects of behavior that will allow us to live a celestial law and thereby to realize our eternal potential and achieve our ultimate happiness. Among the several principles the Lord declares are:

Avoid Light-mindedness: We are reminded to "Sanctify yourselves that your minds become single to God . . . cast away your idle thoughts and your excess of laughter far from you" (vv. 68–69). We are not being asked to live a humorless, crabbed life, but one characterized by reverence and gratitude. We are to treat that which is sacred with respect and "trifle not with sacred things" (D&C 6:12). If we seek first the kingdom of heaven and its righteousness, we will achieve the abundant life.

Avoid Pride: That is, any enmity to God. We are to be humble and repentant and abandon lustful desires and wicked doings (D&C 88:121).

Fast, Pray, Learn: We are to teach one another the doctrine of the kingdom, that all might be edified (see v. 118).

Assemble and Covenant: We are counseled to live in

fellowship and to renew often our covenants with our Heavenly Father (see v. 121).

Avoid Selfishness, Envy, and Coveting: Coveting grows out of base aspirations and false priorities. It is remarkable that the things that men covet most are the most perishable and the least valuable (see v. 123).

Be Actively Engaged in Good Causes: Latter-day Saints must be the "saving leaven" in the communities where they live. Through their good works, others will be led to the truth and to glorify our Father in Heaven.

Charity: We must show love one to another and all mankind.

Be Attentive to the Needs of the Body: Our bodies are the tabernacles of our spirits. We are expected to care for them, for we are engaged in this life not in a short sprint but in a marathon with cosmic consequences. To abuse or to fail to do all that we can to maintain our physical health and strength demonstrates a failure to understand the whole purpose of this mortal existence.

Psychologists have debated which comes first and is most important in shaping the personality—behavior or attitudes. In fact, there is an inextricable relationship between them. Our testimony and knowledge of truth expand as we live what we know, and as our understanding grows, our conduct further changes. Behavior and attitudes, conduct and testimony, goodness and truth interact and reinforce each other.

Christ noted that if one is to know whether the doctrine He taught were of Himself or of He who had sent Him, one must live it (see John 7:16–17). One ultimately comes to know the Father and the Son by behaving in a certain way—which includes keeping the commandments.

Endurance in the grace to which we have been summoned is our fundamental task, but the Lord has warned that a man may fall from grace (see D&C 20:32; 76:31–38; 1 Corinthians 10:12). To have entered into the light and then fallen results in a condition worse than our original fallen state. As the Apostle Peter taught, a man having once disentangled himself from sin, only to become entangled again, will experience an end worse than the beginning. "For it had been better for them not to have known the way of righteousness, than, after they have known it, to turn from the holy commandment delivered unto them" (2 Peter 2:20–21). Brigham Young, who saw many who did not endure, expressed this well:

> Let a man or woman who has received much of the power of God . . . turn away from the holy commandments of the Lord, and it seems that their senses are taken from them, their understanding and judgment in righteousness are taken away, they go into darkness, and become like a blind person who gropes by the wall.[44]

The power of the devil, said President Young, is to "call evil inverted good, or a correct principle made an evil use of."[45] Satan takes the principle of love and transmutes it into lust; he seizes upon faith and changes it into unreflective fanaticism or disillusioned cynicism; he appeals to our hopes and turns them toward imprudence and irresponsibility. The end result is a personality in disintegration, swayed by every trend and doubt.

As Brigham Young also observed, "The difference between God and the Devil is that God creates and organizes, while the whole study of the Devil is to destroy. . . . What, then, is the mission of Satan, that common foe of all the children of men? It is to destroy and make desolate."[46] Or as Lehi declared, Satan "seeketh that all men might be miserable like unto himself" (2 Nephi 2:27).

It is no accident that one of Satan's names is "legion" or "many." Whereas, we refer to the Godhead—and our relation to them—in terms of oneness. There is indeed an integrative quality in godliness, so that one may truly say, "They have it all together." This, finally, is spirituality. Therefore, let us

> *Do what is right, the day-dawn is breaking,*
> *Hailing a future of freedom and light.*[47]

THE SURE FOUNDATIONS OF CHRIST

Paul described Christ as "the author and finisher of our faith" (Hebrews 12:2; see also Moroni 6:4). Happiness, fulfillment, sanctification—spirituality—begins and is accomplished in Him who is the instrument of the Father, Him who made atonement for many, and Him who is our advocate with the Father. The Lamanite prophet Samuel summarized it well:

> For behold, he surely must die that salvation may come; yea, it behooveth him and becometh expedient that he dieth, to bring to pass the resurrection of the dead, that thereby men may be brought into the presence of the Lord. Yea, behold, this death bringeth to pass the resurrection, and redeemeth all mankind from the first death—that spiritual death; for all mankind, by the fall of Adam being cut off from the presence of the Lord, are considered as dead, both as to things temporal and to things spiritual. But behold, the resurrection of Christ redeemeth mankind, yea even all mankind, and bringeth them back into the presence of the Lord. Yea, and it bringeth to pass the condition of repentance, that whosoever repenteth the same is not hewn down and cast into the fire; but

whosoever repenteth not is hewn down and cast into the fire; and there cometh upon them again a spiritual death, yea, a second death, for they are cut off again as to things pertaining to righteousness. [Helaman 14:15–18]

Note that all the elements of our salvation are already fulfilled if we but accept them. But, remember again, we get what we desire. Our desires may be so corrupted that we reject those things pertaining unto righteousness, that is, "the nature of happiness" (Alma 41:11).

One of the characters in C. S. Lewis's *Narnia* tales, Eustace, is turned into a dragon as a result of irresponsibility, childishness, and selfishness. Only through the intervention of Aslan is he transformed not simply back into his human self but into a human that has undergone a "mighty change of heart." After grasping the depth of his own sins and having undergone deep sorrow, Eustace is bidden by Aslan to undress and bathe himself in a well of water. After some perplexity as to what undressing might mean for a dragon, Eustace concludes that it is to scrape off his scales. This he does and steps into the water, but upon emerging from the well, he sees his reflection and sees that another set of scales has appeared. Once again, he scrapes off the scales only to have another set appear. Finally Aslan says that he himself will undress Eustace. Looking with apprehension at the claws of the lion, Eustace finally submits. And, indeed, the claws dig very deep and the pain is very real and the sting of the water is intense when Aslan hurls Eustace into the water—but he emerges no longer a dragon but a real man—man restored, man redeemed, man sanctified.[48]

As Aslan in the myth of *Narnia*, so in life: Christ is the author and finisher of our salvation, our one and only sure foundation. Jacob and Alma, looking forward to the great redemptive act to be performed by the coming Messiah, put the issue not only to their people but to us as well: "Wherefore [there] must needs be an infinite atonement—save it should be an infinite atonement this corruption could not put on incorruption" (2 Nephi 9:7). Alma went on: "Wherefore . . . reconcile yourselves to the will of God, and not to the will of the devil and the flesh; and remember, after ye are reconciled unto God, that it is only in and through the grace of God that ye are saved" (2 Nephi 10:24).

Or as Mosiah put it:

> Marvel not that all mankind, yea, men and women, all nations, kindred, tongues and people, must be born again; yea, born of God, changed from their carnal and fallen state, to a state of righteousness, being redeemed of God, becoming his sons and daughters; And thus they become new creatures; and unless they do this, they can in nowise inherit the kingdom of God. [Mosiah 27:25–26]

Albert Einstein once commented that we cannot solve the problems we now face without changing the way of thinking that caused us to create the problems in the first place.[49] Our problem is the fallen man within. Our destiny is to inherit the divinity within. Whether it be the corruption of society or of our personal ills, the Atonement is the key to bringing about a renewal of our minds and bodies and transforming our understanding, feelings, desires, and behavior. Having thus embraced the truth, with Paul we may then say that we have obtained the "mind of Christ" (1 Corinthians 2:16) and will feel welling up within us the conviction that we are "the temple of God, and that the Spirit of God dwelleth in [us]" (1 Corinthians 3:16).

PART TWO

TRUE CHARACTER

—•—

Commitment and Endurance

How wonderful it is to know a person about whom we almost automatically say, "You can depend on him or her" or, "Her word is her bond." "If I were under fire, that's the man whom I would like in my foxhole." "He or she will always be faithful." "I never have to worry about her." "He is no fair-weather friend."

When we make such comments, we are describing those noble souls who are of such character that, even in dire circumstances, they merit the accolade that they will be true and faithful in all things.

On the other hand, we have all known people who say the right things and give the best public impressions but who are so centered in themselves and so moved by ephemeral feelings and circumstances that no enterprise of moment can be entrusted to them. Such individuals ruin businesses, destroy marriages and families, and engender cynicism in the public square. Incapable of noble commitments, they can nurture no relationship, endure no hardship, or build any lasting achievement. They lack true character.

Some years ago I had the opportunity to fly over the Saudi Arabian desert as a passenger on a C-135 aircraft flying a mission to refuel one of America's most advanced intelligence and communications airplanes. It was a fascinating process to see the "snorkel" extended from our aircraft as we flew above and in tandem with the other airplane. After the fuel had been passed and the refueling line withdrawn, our pilot radioed to the pilot below and said: "We have some VIPs on board. Why don't you fly up a little closer so they can get a better look?" I was surprised, for we seemed already pretty close; I felt as though I could almost reach out and touch the other plane. Nevertheless, the other plane began to ascend. Suddenly one of our party shouted, "They're going to hit us!" Apparently the other pilot and ours realized at the same moment that disaster was imminent. Our pilot veered our plane to the left, while the other pilot turned his plane to the right . . . but too late. Our right wing and his left wing collided. The other aircraft disappeared over the horizon and ours lost power in one half of the aircraft. Then the pilot simply said to us, "You're going to be alright, but. . . ." *But*—surely the most terrifying word in any language! He then explained that we might have to ditch the plane and parachute out. I remember asking, "You mean from up here?!"

Many years prior to this incident, we were all gathered in a great premortal council. Our Father explained that, in order for us to realize our divine potential and progress toward becoming like Him, we would have to be born into mortality. I can almost hear Him say, "And you're going to be alright, but . . ." In the next chapters we are going to consider what follows the *but*. What are some of the challenges we face and what do we need to do in order to meet them?

I will argue that the key to whom we become—our

character—and how well we meet both the challenges and opportunities of life—our endurance—depend on the nature and depth of our commitments. It is the making and keeping of sacred covenants that shape our very nature and allow us not only to withstand challenges but also to triumph over them.

As to the incident over the Saudi desert, yes, my fellow travelers and I did make it safely down to the ground. In the same way, as we hold fast to sacred covenants, we shall make it safely back into the presence of our Heavenly Father.

CHAPTER 3

Glorified in Truth:
Character and Consequences

When I was a young professor at the University of Virginia, I was befriended by a very distinguished senior colleague, Alpheus Mason. As an expert in constitutional law, over his career he had taught many students, some of whom had become famous jurists. I asked him what he had learned in all those years of teaching many thousands of students. He responded, as always, in brief and direct form: "Character is more important than intellect."

What is this trait that Professor Mason so highly prized? The word *character* comes from the Greek *charassein,* meaning to engrave. Hence, as Professor Mason meant it, an individual with character is one whose personality is distinguished by or engraved with moral excellence and firmness.

As an example, consider Harry Potter in *Harry Potter and the Chamber of Secrets.* Dumbledore, the headmaster of Harry's school, notes that when Harry Potter was a child, the boy had been attacked and scarred by the wicked but brilliant Lord Voldemort. In the encounter, Voldemort had inadvertently transferred some of his own powers or abilities to Harry. Harry feared that he might thus be like Voldemort, but Dumbledore assured him: "It is our choices, Harry, that show what we truly are, far more than our abilities."[50]

Making correct choices and enduring in our commitment therein is the essence of true character.

In the law there are two contrasting ways of looking at commitment. The first is that we scrupulously honor our commitments (*Pacta Sunt Servanda*), and the second is that our commitments remain binding only so long as the circumstances that gave rise to those commitments remain the same (*Rebus Sic Stanibus*).

In His wisdom and dealings with us, the Lord has transcended this apparent contradiction in human law. He speaks of the "new and everlasting covenant" and invites us to enter and endure in that covenant of the gospel with all its associated commitments. Being grounded in the established purpose of bringing to pass the immortality and eternal life of man, that covenant transcends yet responds to changing circumstances.

Although the terms of the gospel covenant are fixed by God, man is free to accept or reject the covenant. But, once having accepted the commitment and bending all our efforts to keep it, we are assured by God that He will be our Lord and Master and will assist us in all the travails and opportunities of our life. When we call, He will answer. He, being our Lord, helps us to master circumstances and control passions rather than be swept away by them. Otherwise, we are left to our own devices. God will not compel the human mind or will. But as we keep the terms of the covenant, our character will be decisively shaped, and we will show forth and grow in the image of Christ; the engraving of our character will be that of eternity. We literally grow into the image of the Savior who is our Master.

Can you therefore see why our Heavenly Father has spoken in

the harshest terms of covenant-breakers, those who are faithless in keeping their covenants? There is a dramatic example of this recorded by Luke in the Acts of the Apostles. In the communal life of those early-day Saints, the followers of Christ pooled their resources in order to support one another. A certain man named Ananias and his wife, Sapphira, sold a possession, and under the terms of the covenant were obliged to lay the proceeds before the apostles for distribution. They did so, but gave only a portion of the price to the apostles with the impression, however, that they had dedicated everything. In effect, they sought to deceive.

Peter noted that the property was indeed theirs to dispose of as they would, but that they had willfully lied, as he said, "Why hast thou conceived this thing in thine heart? Thou hast not lied unto men, but unto God." Being so accused, Ananias fell to the floor dead, as did his wife when she was later confronted with their conspiracy (see Acts 5:1–10). I don't suppose Luke could have given a more striking incident of the importance of truthfully making and keeping covenants than this one!

In baptism we associate ourselves with the new and everlasting covenant, exhibiting faith in Christ unto repentance, ever keeping before us His great atonement, loving Him because He loved us first (see 1 John 4:15), taking His name upon us, keeping His commandments. As a result, we receive the gift of the Holy Ghost, who serves as witness, comforter, guide, and teacher. In the house of the Lord, the temples, we progress in the new and everlasting covenant by our commitment to fidelity, sacrifice, service, and consecration; and in the work of the temple associate ourselves with Christ as saviors upon the mount of Zion. We are blessed by our faithfulness and service with an endowment of power—power to overcome the evils of this world, to receive the blessings of an eternal family, and to be immersed in the glory of God.

The implications are clear: when we seek to meet the challenges of life and the variability of circumstances, we must consult and be guided by our eternal purposes and solemn covenants. Whether it be in family, at work or play, at home or abroad, in good times or bad, if we let the gospel covenant guide our lives, our lives will be touched with grace and all the purposes of our creation fulfilled.

This is not the way of the world. The world entices us to let circumstances—subject to ephemeral feeling, sudden passions, and the gusts of changing social winds—guide our choices and inspire our actions. If we follow the way of the world and allow ourselves to be as children, "tossed to and fro, and carried about with every wind of doctrine, by the sleight of men, and cunning craftiness, whereby they lie in wait to deceive" (Ephesians 4:14), whatever our intellect, however powerful our abilities, we shall shrink and diminish.

Do you recall the drama *A Man for All Seasons,* which chronicles the struggle between Henry VIII and Sir Thomas More? On one occasion, an ambitious but morally ungrounded young man, Richard Rich, seeks and is refused employment by Sir Thomas. Richard Rich protests that he would be steadfast, to which Sir Thomas replies, "Richard, you couldn't answer for yourself even so far as tonight."[51] Indeed, those who have departed from fidelity to covenants and let momentary circumstances determine their actions lack the steadfastness that would allow them to stand in the storms of life.

In the musical *Camelot,* we hear the words, "Do not let your passions destroy your dreams."[52] Indeed, he who responds to the challenges of marriage and family and the difficulties of mortality by retreating from his covenants or who seizes, in violation of solemn covenants, opportunities for gain or fame or even convenience, will at last not only destroy his dreams but also surrender his eternal destiny.

Ultimately, the development and manifestation of character is a question of integrity. To have integrity implies not only being whole and complete, but having it all together and possessing a willingness to seek the truth, to follow the truth discovered, and to bear witness of it in all times and in all places. A profoundly good person is one who is grounded in the truth.

As earlier discussed, the Lord has declared that "truth is knowledge of things as they are, and as they were, and as they are to come" (D&C 93:24). In that same section, the Savior declared that those who keep the commandments will be "glorified in truth" and that He, Christ, is "the true light that lighteth every man that cometh into the world" (vv. 28, 2).

The ancient Greek philosopher Aristotle defined nature, including human nature, in a most interesting way, one very compatible with the teachings of the 93rd section of the Doctrine and Covenants. He argued that what is natural should not be seen from a statistical point of view, that is, counting what people actually do and justifying behavior on the basis that "everyone is doing it." Rather it should be seen from a teleological (from the Greek word *telos,* purpose or end) point of view. We should look to the true potential and thus destiny of an individual to determine if he or she is acting "naturally," that is, in accord with one's proper end.

Aristotle gave an analogy of an acorn and observed that the true nature or purpose (telos) of an acorn can only be realized by its growing into a tall, straight, and mighty oak. If it lacks proper sun and nourishment or is located under a cliff so that it must bend, it will never grow into what it potentially could. And, if an oak had feelings, it would never know true "happiness." And so it is, said Aristotle, with human beings.[53]

Of all the truths we must know, the truth about ourselves is most crucial—where we came from, why we are here, and where we are going. When I was growing up, there came a moment in high school when a friend and I discovered that there was something more interesting than basketball—girls. One day we spoke to our seminary teacher about dating and what would be appropriate behavior, asking in effect what would be the "lines" in our conduct. Being a wise teacher, Brother Irwin Wirkus said, "I'm not going to define for you where the edge of the precipice is, but I will tell you who you are and then you must decide how you should act in accord with that understanding." He expounded the plan of salvation more eloquently than I had ever heard. He taught us the true identity of these girls we would be dating and also helped us understand who we were in eternal terms. In doing so, he placed a greater charge upon us than if he had tried to draw lines. He taught us about a life of truth and consequences. Echoed in his teachings was the commission given by the resurrected Lord to the Nephites: "Therefore, what manner of men ought ye to be? Verily I say unto you, even as I am" (3 Nephi 27:27).

As philosophers and prophets alike have declared, incorrect understanding leads to inappropriate actions—which in turn lead to unhappiness. As Alma explained to Corianton: "Wickedness never was happiness" (Alma 41:10). After observing the grief that had come upon his people, Mormon momentarily hoped that they would draw the conclusion that their behavior had ended in misery. But, alas, such was not to be. As he wrote:

> And it came to pass that when I, Mormon, saw their lamentation and their mourning and their sorrow before

the Lord, my heart did begin to rejoice within me, knowing the mercies and the long-suffering of the Lord, therefore supposing that he would be merciful unto them that
they would again become a righteous people.

But behold this my joy was vain, for their sorrowing
was not unto repentance, because of the goodness of God;
but it was rather the sorrowing of the damned, because
the Lord would not always suffer them to take happiness
in sin. (Mormon 2:12–13)

Again, both prophets and philosophers have observed that
though all men desire happiness, the acquisition of lasting happiness depends on our understanding, our knowledge of truth, and
our obedience to what we sometimes call doctrine and principles.
As we have seen, how we think shapes our actions, and our actions
determine our happiness.

When I was young there was a program on the radio called
"Truth or Consequences." It was a quiz show in which if the
contestant failed to correctly answer a question, he or she would
have to suffer some unpleasant consequence. Whether they knew
it or not, the writers of the program were dialed in to an eternal
principle. The things we do, good or bad, all have a consequence.

I spent part of my professional life studying and developing
military defense strategies. We used gaming and simulation in this
effort in which we would identify goals, values, interests, and
desired outcomes, then construct scenarios (a hypothetical series
of events) that might challenge those values and interests—and
then allow students to decide what steps to take. If they were to
be successful, the players had to make clear choices and have the
imagination to determine the likely consequences of their choices.

As Moses said to the children of Israel:

See, I have set before thee this day life and good, and death and evil; In that I command thee this day to love the Lord thy God, to walk in his ways, and to keep his commandments and his statutes and his judgments, that thou mayest live and multiply: and the Lord thy God shall bless thee in the land whither thou goest to possess it. . . . I call heaven and earth to record this day against you, that I have set before you life and death, blessing and cursing; therefore choose life, that both thou and thy seed may live. [Deuteronomy 30:15–16, 19]

Or in Joshua's words: "Choose you this day whom ye will serve" (Joshua 24:15).

And yet many resist clear choices—not realizing that this will not relieve them from the deadly effects of their own hesitancy. One may seek to escape the responsibility of moral agency, but the inexorable workings of cause and effect continue. There is the story of Pat, known for a somewhat casual approach to the counsels of heaven, who is now lying on his death bed. To the charge of the priest to "renounce the devil and all his works," Pat replies, "Father, I'm in no condition to offend anyone at this point!"

Choices do have consequences, an accumulated impact over time that operates like compound interest. We must look not only at the immediate impact but at the train of events and outcomes that will follow from our choices.

Do you recall the cartoon *Calvin and Hobbes* by Bill Watterson? Calvin, a very precocious little boy, had a friend, a stuffed tiger called Hobbes. But, although his parents could not see it, Hobbes was very much alive, ready to pounce on Calvin at any moment. In a cartoon of some years ago, Calvin and Hobbes are rolling down a hill in their wagon with ever-accelerating speed.

Calvin looks back at Hobbes and says, "Ever notice how decisions make chain reactions?"

"How so?" asks Hobbes.

Calvin responds: "Well, each decision we make determines the range of choices we'll face next. Take this fork in the road, for instance. Which way should we go? Arbitrarily I choose left. Now as a direct result of that decision, we're faced with another choice: should we jump this ledge or ride along the side of it? If we hadn't turned left at the fork, this new choice would never have come up."

At this point, Hobbes exclaims, "I note with some dismay you've chosen to jump the ledge."

Now hurtling through the air, Calvin yells, "Right, and that decision will give us new choices."

Hobbes dryly remarks, "Like should we bail out or die in the landing?"

"Exactly," observes Calvin, "Our first decision created a chain reaction of decisions. LET'S JUMP!"

Both land in a stream and, with water running down his face, Calvin concludes, "See? If you don't make each decision carefully, you never know *where* you'll end up. That's an important lesson we should learn sometime."

To which Hobbes wearily responds, "I wish we could talk about these things without the visual aids!"[54]

Consider Shakespeare's *Macbeth:* Honored by his countrymen for his leading and courageous part in the defense of his good king and native land, Macbeth was a man of affection and conscience. He saw himself as basically a good man. But he was also a man of ambition, an ambition that turned murderous. He formed the idea of killing the king and assuming the throne. He was both attracted by the prospect of sovereign sway and repelled by the bloody plan he had conceived in order to achieve this preeminence.

Bolstered in his evil resolve by his wife, he carried out the crime, claiming indifference to his immortal destiny if he could but realize his earthly ambition. And yet he executed the sanguinary deed in deep anguish of conscience.

However, having finally translated the treacherous thought into violent act, thereby putting his immortal soul in jeopardy, he became increasingly determined and paranoid about keeping secure his ill-gotten kingship. All was eventually swallowed up in his egoism, his absolute concern for self, so much so that he declared:

> *For mine own good,*
> *All causes shall give way.*[55]

So focused was he on himself that he ultimately came to believe that should he be overthrown, the whole world would be overthrown with him. Indeed, his corruption infected all the land, sowing disarray, suspicion, and fear. And, when he finally forfeited not only his soul but his earthly gains as well, he, in his egoism, concluded that all life is

> *. . . a tale*
> *Told by an idiot,*
> *full of sound and fury,*
> *Signifying nothing.*[56]

It was not life that had been diminished to nothing, but Macbeth himself. Where he had once worn his greatness as a noble giant, the consequences of his selfish acts had, in the bard's words, reduced Macbeth to a "dwarfed thief."

Although Macbeth's sins were full of blood, the process of his corruption stands as a warning to every man and woman. We form in our minds unworthy thoughts and then with troubled consciences enact the thoughts. But, although we may initially clearly distinguish in our minds between good and evil, to justify ourselves, we finally build an edifice of lies, of equivocation, of degrading acts—until our sense of right and wrong is stilled, until we become the entire universe, until that universe dwindles into bitter insignificance.

Both Alma and Amulek undoubtedly had this spiral of degradation in mind when they counseled us not to procrastinate the day of our repentance (see Alma 13:27; 34:33–35). For the night comes. But the night comes not simply with the grave but the darkness that enshrouds us in this life as the Holy Ghost departs and the Light of Christ is extinguished. As Amulek so chillingly declared, we become "subjected to the spirit of the devil, and he doth seal you his; therefore, the Spirit of the Lord hath withdrawn from you, and hath no place in you, and the devil hath all power over you; and this is the final state of the wicked" (Alma 34:35).

Alexander Pope described this insidious process in his oft-quoted lines:

> Vice is a monster of so frightful mien,
> As, to be hated, needs but to be seen;
> Yet seen too oft, familiar with her face,
> We first endure, then pity, then embrace.[57]

If unworthy thoughts and acts generate more unworthy thoughts and acts—with the accompanying deadening of conscience—so worthy thoughts and acts have opposite effects. As Nephi declared, concerning the working of the Liahona in the Book of Mormon, "Thus we see that by small means the Lord can bring about great things" (1 Nephi 16:29). Just as gluttony and smoking yield one result, so proper diet and exercise yield another. Likewise, as ignoble thoughts and acts yield one result, so worthy thoughts and small acts of kindness yield another. And in both cases, the consequences are cumulative and exponential, that is, there is a snowball effect.

All the things that happen in time, such as temporal matters, have eternal or spiritual consequences; which is to say, they imprint themselves upon the immortal soul. They shape character. It is thus that we grow into the image of Christ. True character is not an interlude or spectacular moment in our lives but the very fabric of our lives. Faithfulness to sacred covenants is not an experience or happening but a mode of life, a search after the mind and will of God and a determination to follow that mind and will.

To break the cycle of corruption or to initiate the cycle of sanctification requires an act of discipline, born of faith in Christ unto repentance and ultimately rewarded with an endowment of grace. The cycle of sanctification depends on a conversion, a turning about, a renewed mind and heart, a birth into newness of life.

In a general priesthood meeting, President David O. McKay spoke of his boyhood desire to have a vision comparable to that of the boy prophet, Joseph Smith. But an epiphany eluded him in his youth. Nonetheless, he knew what was true and right and acted accordingly. He served a mission, he consecrated his life to God and his fellowman, and he became a noble husband and father. And at last he said: "The spiritual manifestation for which I had prayed as a boy . . . came as a natural sequence to the performance of duty."[58]

I was in the assembly where President McKay dedicated the London Temple. I was sitting on the front row of the temple chapel awaiting President McKay and his party, when suddenly I felt impelled to rise to my feet, tears welling up in my eyes. To my surprise everyone arose as one, exhibiting the same emotion as I. Then President McKay came into view as he walked from around the podium. Spontaneously the congregation began to sing, "We Thank Thee, O God, for a Prophet."[59] His whole being was suffused with light. He showed forth the decorum of eternity without fanaticism or display. The Lord was revealed through him. It was clear that through a lifetime performance of duty, David O. McKay not only knew of Christ but knew Christ.

Life is a becoming. We were sent into mortality to become like Christ. We must, therefore, keep this image ever before us and, in every act of life, choose so as to realize this image. To each of us who so strive, the Lord has promised:

> For all who will have a blessing at my hands shall abide the law which was appointed for that blessing, and the conditions thereof, as were instituted from before the foundation of the world. . . . For I am the Lord thy God, and will be with thee even unto the end of the world, and through all eternity; for verily I seal upon you your exaltation, and prepare a throne for you in the kingdom of my Father, with Abraham your father. [D&C 132:5, 49]

We often speak of faith in Christ as the ability to both believe in Him and believe Him, in effect, a confidence to rely on Him. When we speak of our being faithful, on the other hand, we refer to the fact that He can rely on us. Character finally refers to the ability to endure in our commitments long after the excitement that gave rise to the commitments is past. It is to those of such diligence that the Lord promises "his fulness" and "his glory." As the Lord declared, they are they who "shall overcome all things" and become "just men made perfect through Jesus the mediator of the new covenant" (D&C 76:56, 60, 69). Old or young, may we be true servants, youth of the noble birthright, honest in all our dealings, true to the gospel light—that we may be one of those described by the Apostle John, who will recognize Christ when He appears, for "we shall be like him" (1 John 3:2).

CHAPTER 4

For It Must Needs Be:
Not Easy but Worth It

"And we know that all things work together for good
to them that love God" (Romans 8:28)

On 20 July 1966, Ed Hubbard's life was decisively changed. In the morning, there was no hot water, and he had only a stale donut and cold eggs to eat—which he decided to skip. Before that day was over, he would be shot down over North Vietnam and become a prisoner of war for the next seven years. He later told me that while there, he decided that every day thereafter was going to be a "good day."

It is wrong to assume that the more righteous one is, or the more diligently one strives to keep his or her covenants with the Lord, the less suffering one will have to endure. The promise is that he or she will be blessed, though the blessing may be the strength to endure suffering. All suffer—the just and the unjust. But the unjust live as well with the consequences of their own sins.

This is the way life is arranged. God does not sit around wondering what test to throw up before you next. Such tests are integral to life—they go with the territory. Father Lehi understood this truth:

For it must needs be, that there is an opposition in all things. If not so . . . righteousness could not be brought to pass, neither wickedness, neither holiness nor misery, neither good nor bad. Wherefore, all things must needs be a compound in one. [2 Nephi 2:11]

Go back in imagination to the great premortal council, convened before the earth was created. Mortality was there explained as a necessary condition for perfectibility, that is, to become like our Father in Heaven. Three critical aspects of this mortal condition were to be:

The challenge of sustaining life
The challenge of enduring others' choices
The challenge of making our own choices

Satan elucidated the negative implications of these challenges and offered:

Escape from want and pain
Escape from the burdens of freedom

Perhaps you can see why one-third of the host of heaven were persuaded by Satan's approach and said, "No thanks!" to the plan of salvation.

We, however, wanting the achievement, yes, the glory, said, "Let's go for it!" We who are here accepted life without accepting the escapes that Satan offered. We understood, at least abstractly, that life would be difficult and at times, excruciatingly painful. And yet, it is recorded that we shouted for joy. We should, therefore, consider not only the trials of mortality but the joys. But to know those joys, we must avoid wishful thinking—wishing that mortality were something other than it is, along the line of fairy-tales, "We were born and lived happily ever after." On the other hand, we must eschew fear and fearful behavior. As Christ said, "Let not your heart be troubled, neither let it be afraid" (John 14:27). Rather, as Nephi taught, we should live "with a steadfastness in Christ, having a perfect brightness of hope" (2 Nephi 31:20).

If we are to both endure and prosper, we must get our assumptions correct: life *is* a challenge; it's supposed to be. God seldom, if ever, manufactures troubles. They are inherent in the nature of mortality and of agency. And the joy that Father Lehi said was the object of mortal existence, arises from a proper understanding of this life and a proper approach to it.

The British theologian Richard Whately (1787–1863) grasped well this point when he remarked that "happiness is no laughing matter."[60] Do you recall those great lines from the musical *Teahouse of the August Moon?*

> *Pain makes men think.*
> *Thought makes men wise.*
> *Wisdom makes life endurable.*[61]

Cervantes, the author of *Don Quixote,* said, "No man is born wise."[62] It is in the clash with our diverse realities and the way we seek to cope with those realities through the choices we make, that wisdom, if it is to be attained at all, comes. Ultimately, that wisdom is to know the mind of God.

Thinking and choosing, while glorious, are also serious matters. For choice to be genuine, the paths that we and others take must entail different values and produce different outcomes. Very often, choices require trade-offs among apparently good things and among projected different costs and benefits. At the heart of real choice is always the reality that there are no free lunches. This was the dilemma that Adam and Eve at last faced in the Garden of Eden. The complex process of evaluating alternatives and living with the consequences is the very essence of freedom.

The fortunate misfortune of this is that, in a society of men and women, each endowed with the potential to choose, each of us must cope with other peoples' choices, including those that might do us harm or in fact restrict our own freedom of action. And yet, any attempt by Divinity to prevent on a regular basis the negative consequences of wicked or foolish choices of any one of us would finally negate everyone's freedom. The tares must be allowed to grow if the wheat is to come to full maturity.

Some time ago, I met another man who had been a prisoner of war in Vietnam, Captain Charles Plumb, who often made a presentation called *Prison Thinking*. Shot down, captured, tortured, and confined to an eight-foot cell, he finally came in contact with Book Shumaker, the first American that he had seen since his ordeal began. Shumaker asked him how things were going. His remarks, perhaps understandably so, were bitter and sarcastic, to which Book Shumaker replied, "You've got an attitude problem!" And, indeed, Charles Plumb decided that he did. He outlined in the book he subsequently wrote three things people typically do as they confront trouble: pity themselves, blame everyone else, and become bitter against life. Captain Plumb told me that he had resolved that he couldn't give way to bitterness because "bitterness kills me. It doesn't hurt anyone else around me. Not being bitter is a survival technique." I suspect this is one reason why the Lord taught us to: "Love your enemies, bless them that curse you, do good to them that hate you, and pray for them which despitefully use you, and persecute you" (Matthew 5:44).

As we adopt Plumb's approach, we not only control our reactions to our environment, but we begin to shape that environment. Think for a moment of your response to people who are bathed in self-pity and bitterness. Unfortunately perhaps, such attitudes seldom evoke positive assistance or change. There was a famous character in Al Capp's cartoon, *Lil' Abner,* who was so negative and miserable that he carried his own rain cloud with him. And in Milton's *Paradise Lost,* Satan bemoans that no matter where he goes, hell is there, for he carries hell with him.[63] Indeed, he *is* hell. And so it can be with us.

But there is also a difference between the suffering of the righteous and that of the wicked. The Apostle Paul distinguished between trials that are godly, that is sanctifying and hence beneficial, and those trials that cause worldly sorrow, which results in bitterness, alienation from God and fellowman, and death even in the midst of life (see 2 Corinthians 7:10). Recall once again Mormon's words concerning the horror brought upon his people, largely by their own actions:

> When I, Mormon, saw their lamentation and their mourning and their sorrow before the Lord, my heart did begin to rejoice within me, knowing the mercies and the long-suffering of the Lord, therefore supposing that he would be merciful unto them that they would again become a righteous people. But behold this my joy was vain, for their sorrowing was not unto repentance, because of the goodness of God; but it was rather the sorrowing of the damned, because the Lord would not always suffer them to take happiness in sin. [Mormon 2:12–13]

Those who are faithful to their covenants are assured that they will not have to suffer in vain. There are two reasons for this, both of which are based on the mission of the Savior: First, He did not come to eliminate suffering but, rather, to turn into joy all suffering that has to be endured: "Blessed are they that mourn: for they shall be comforted" (Matthew 5:4). Second, He came that suffering might result not only in good but in perfection. In this, Christ is our model: "Though he were a Son, yet learned he obedience by the things which he suffered; And being made perfect, he became the author of eternal salvation unto all them that obey him" (Hebrews 5:8–9).

These outcomes are possible because the righteous are drawn to God and sustained by Him in their trials. The Prophet Joseph Smith taught that as one proves he is willing to serve God in all circumstances, an assurance is given that is "an anchor to the soul, sure and steadfast. Though the thunders might roll and lightnings flash, and earthquakes bellow, and war gather thick around, yet this hope and knowledge [will] support the soul in every hour of trial, trouble and tribulation."[64]

Mortality was designed to provide the children of God with necessary experience. One can benefit from such experience only by going through it. But the righteous have the assurance that they can receive the strength necessary to endure whatever comes upon them, and thus their experience will work for their eternal good. This is what Paul meant when he wrote in his epistle to the Romans: "And we know that all things work together for good to them that love God" (Romans 8:28). The Lord reiterated this principle in this dispensation when he declared: "And all things wherewith you have been afflicted shall work together for your good" (D&C 98:3).

A Multitude of Troubles

There are trials and troubles—and then there are trials and troubles! Although mortality in itself carries an abundance of challenges, not all challenges are of the same nature. For our purposes, let me lump together a number of ills, different kinds of sorrows and affliction, into three broad categories:

1. Unavoidable (for all practical purposes) ills—largely outside our control—general or natural or social causes: endowments of birth, aging, much illness, economic depression, war, earthquakes, and the like; ills originating in the perverse or careless behavior of others.

2. Ills of judgment—Trust misplaced, risk or cost underestimated, alternative courses of action not developed, insufficient information—sheer stupidity. As Talleyrand said, "This is worse than a crime, it's a blunder!"[65]

3. Ills of disobedience—We do not entirely understand the basis of all our trials. There is a complexity of immediate and distant causes and a limit to all our human explanation. Hence, the wise counsel found on the wall of the Memorial Chapel at Stanford University: "There is no narrowing so deadly as the narrowing of man's horizon of spiritual things. No worse evil could befall him on his course on earth than to lose sight of heaven. . . . No widening of science, no possession of abstract of truth, can indemnify for an enfeebled hold on the highest and central truths of humanity."[66]

We must not deal with our trials by a passive retreat from a life of commitment and engagement or by cynical detachment. We have essentially two tasks: to sanctify and to be sanctified by those ills we cannot banish and to avoid or escape those ills we can.

PART TWO

SANCTIFICATION IN SUFFERING

If we are truly to follow in the way of the poor wayfaring man of grief, can we really expect to escape the trials of what appears to be an unjust reality? As Peter wrote:

> For this is thankworthy, if a man for conscience toward God endure grief, suffering wrongfully. For what glory is it, if, when ye be buffeted for your faults, ye shall take it patiently? but if, when ye do well, and suffer for it, ye take it patiently, this is acceptable with God. For even hereunto were ye called: because Christ also suffered for us, leaving us an example, that ye should follow his steps: Who did no sin, neither was guile found in his mouth: Who, when he was reviled, reviled not again; when he suffered, he threatened not; but committed himself to him that judgeth righteously: Who his own self bare our sins in his own body on the tree, that we, being dead to sins, should live unto righteousness: by whose stripes ye were healed. [1 Peter 2:19–24]

In coping with these unavoidable trials, understand this:

• God cares. He feels our suffering; He seeks to help us escape unnecessary pain; but He seeks also to preserve our ability to grow unto divinity.

• We should care: To relieve our own pain, we must reach out to alleviate others' sorrows. The Apostle James speaks of true religion as reaching out to comfort and sustain others (see James 1:37). And King Benjamin observed that, if we are in the service of our fellow beings, we are in the service of God (see Mosiah 2:17). We are counseled by Alma that we who are come into the fold of God are "to be called his people, and are willing to bear one another's burdens, that they may be light; Yea, and are willing to mourn with those that mourn; yea, and comfort those that stand in need of comfort, and to stand as witnesses of God at all times and in all things, and in all places that [we] may be in, even unto death, that [we] may be redeemed of God, and be numbered with those of the first resurrection, that [we] may have eternal life" (Mosiah 18:8–9).

Whatever our personal troubles or fears, we may rise above them only by orienting ourselves to others. In the words of Jesus: "He that findeth his life shall lose it: and he that loseth his life for my sake shall find it" (Matthew 10:39).

AVOIDING OR ESCAPING SUFFERING

As the seventeenth-century French moralist and writer Jean de la Bruyère (1645–1696) observed, "The majority of men devote the greater part of their lives to making their remaining years unhappy."[67] When I was serving as a young bishop in Charlottesville, Virginia, my first counselor and I were visiting with a woman who had complicated her life beyond belief through disobeying the commands of God. Upon leaving her, I turned to my counselor and said, quite inelegantly, but quite genuinely, "Sin just isn't worth the hassle."

I suspect that this was what Alma had in mind when he declared that "wickedness never was happiness" (Alma 41:10). Remember once again the words of King Arthur in the musical *Camelot:* "We must not let our passions destroy our dreams." Nor must we ever be possessed by our possessions.

The path of safety lies in the following principles:

• In obedience—submitting our will to God's

• In sacrifice—giving up our "precious sins," all those things we prefer to the Kingdom of God

• In living the law of the gospel—becoming peacemakers, pure in heart, merciful, meek, bearing each others' burdens and bringing comfort;

• In maintaining fidelity to others—including sexual fidelity in the marriage bond and guarding the fount of life;

• In consecrating—to give self to others and to the establishment of the Kingdom of God.

All this depends on faith in Christ and entails true repentance. As Paul wrote: "For Godly sorrow worketh repentance to salvation not to be repented of: but the sorrow of the world worketh death." Or as it is translated in the New English Bible: "For the wound which is borne in God's way brings a change of heart too salutary to regret; but the hurt which is borne in the world's way brings death" (2 Corinthians 7:10).

ON FEAR

At both the birth of Jesus and in His final meeting with His apostles, the proclamation of peace and the banishment of fear were proclaimed: "And they were sore afraid. And the angel said unto them, fear not" (Luke 2:9–10). "Let not your heart be troubled, neither let it be afraid" (John 14:27).

A life filled with challenges, frustrations, difficulties, and at times real pain can cause us to experience fear, anxiety, and a troubled heart. President David O. McKay, speaking at the 1958 dedication of the London Temple, spoke of fears and anxieties that grip all mankind and said that such worries are inspired by that same being who, in the premortal council, promised us a mortal existence void of pain and fear.

How do we deal with such fears without abandoning the challenges of mortality? How are we to know hope and peace? It should be noted, first of all, that some fears, like pain or guilt, may be warning signals that may cause us to avoid or eschew real dangers to our well-being. A life of absolute ease and a life with no fears are neither to be expected nor, from the point of view of our growth, to be welcomed. However, many of our fears stem from our misunderstanding of the nature of mortality and an inability to harmonize our will with His, He who is the creator of time. With that understanding and the willingness to follow Christ in faith, it is possible to be animated by hope and to be at peace even in the midst of turmoil. Within that context, let me suggest several strategies for avoiding fear:

Make Defensive Preparations. It is impossible to predict the future with certitude. But we can take measures to cushion the blows of fate, and we can compose our inner being so as not to be defeated by those blows. In the Doctrine and Covenants the Lord counsels, "If ye are prepared ye shall not fear" (D&C 38:30), and "Fear not thine enemies" (D&C 136:17). Indeed, the Lord further states that we should not fear "man more than God" (D&C 3:7) and commands that we should "fear not to do good" (D&C 6:33). The prophets have consistently explained both the temporal and the spiritual preparations we should make in order to endure the "slings and arrows of outrageous fortune."

Make Proper Use of Our Present Circumstances. Even the ancient pagan philosophers understood that happiness is not determined by that which surrounds us but rather by that which is within us. The great first-century Greek historian and essayist Plutarch observed that a key to contented living is having the ability to take the circumstances of our lives, magnifying that which edifies while reducing the impact of the negative. This depends less on what is happening to us than who we are. As he observed:

> It is the shoe that bends along with the foot, not the other way around; and likewise . . . dispositions mould life. . . . It follows that we should purify our innate well of contentment and then external things will be in harmony with us, too. . . . It is our job, if we are sensible, to accommodate ourselves to whatever fortune deals us and to allocate everything to a place where, as each situation arises, if it is congruent, we can maximize its benefits, and if it is unwelcome, we can minimize its harm.[68]

Do Not Be Controlled by Others' Moods and Behavior. This is perhaps one of the reasons we are told to forgive. Again, Plutarch wrote that "Fortune can make us fall ill, can deprive us of our wealth, can ruin our relationship with the people or the king, but it cannot make someone who is good, brave and high-minded into a bad, cowardly, mean-spirited, petty and spiteful person, and it cannot deprive us of the permanent presence of an attitude towards life which is a more helpful guide in this sphere than a helmsman is on a sea voyage."[69]

Avoid Excessive or Unsupported Desires. Recall again Lowell Thomas's observation that many people in the hunt of life desire to bag an elephant but are oft disappointed when they get the squirrels instead. Of course, they have failed to arm themselves with elephant guns, to go where elephants are, to aim at an elephant, and then to pull the trigger! We fear failure, but we sometimes fail to prepare for success. However, we sometimes define success in ways that are unworthy, inappropriate for our talents and callings, or demanding of false priorities. Even if we attain our desires in such circumstances, we are gripped with the fear that we may have missed the mark of life.

Make the Atonement and Faith in Christ the Anchor of Our Life. Jesus Christ is the foundation of all our strategies of contentment, and He it is who gives substance to our hopes.

Moses described apostate Israel as a nation no longer grounded on the rock of salvation, the Holy One of Israel:

> The sword without, and terror within, shall destroy both the young man and the virgin, the suckling also with the man of gray hairs. . . . For they are a nation void of counsel, neither is there any understanding in them. O that they were wise, that they understood this, that they would consider their latter end. [Deuteronomy 32:25, 28–29]

And the Lord has spoken to us in latter days: "Learn of me, and listen to my words: walk in the meekness of my Spirit, and you shall have peace in me" (D&C 19:23).

On Joy

So, at last, in the trials of this mortal existence, what are we to expect? Joy!

Lehi said that "Men are, that they might have joy" (2 Nephi 2:25), and Joseph Smith taught that "Happiness is the object and design of our existence."[70] The object of mortality, then, is not to be miserable. Yet, in the midst of our trials, many of us have concluded that the joy of life will come only after we have passed the tests of this life and crossed beyond the veil. Indeed, many have taken comfort in this proposition by portraying Christ Himself as a "man of sorrows." Great sorrow He did suffer. But there is nothing in scripture that indicates that He did not enjoy mortality or that He counted His life as miserable.

I would counsel that we not become so overwhelmed by our challenges, so distracted by the darkness, that we miss the joys of the present life, the glories of mortality.

There are, I think, three keys to obtaining present joy. They are related to the ways we avoid being fearful.

1. Gratitude
2. Repentance
3. Service

Gratitude

Few things are as beneficial as having a grateful heart. Amulek plead with the Zormaites "that ye contend no more against the Holy Ghost, but that ye receive [Him], and take upon you the name of Christ; that ye humble yourselves . . . and worship God in whatsoever place ye may be in, in spirit and in truth; and that ye live in thanksgiving daily, for the many mercies and blessings which He doth bestow upon you" (Alma 34:38).

Let me share with you some items in my personal bag of gratitude and happiness:

Sight and Sound: What a marvelous product of our electronic age is the little instrument we call the iPod. At minimal cost and less inconvenience, we can travel to the Grand Ole Opry with the Judds and to the city of Berlin to hear Leonard Bernstein conduct Beethoven's Ninth Symphony, "Ode to Joy."

I once gave a Walkman to my father, who had a hearing loss. At about the same time, he also had cataracts removed from his eyes. My, how he appreciated what he heard and what he saw. His patriarchal blessing had promised that he would live so long as life was sweet to him. He took this to mean that to live life is to seek the sweet in life.

Language and Speech: I am further grateful for the wonder of speech and communication. Many have noted that it is speech that reinforces our humanity and reflects the potential of our divinity. How I love the cadences, the shades, the sounds of speech as they communicate the deepest joys, desires, insights, hopes, fears, and challenges of immortal man traveling along the path of mortality. I have, for instance, been thrilled by the poetic language of William Wordsworth's stirring depiction of the cycle of life in his celebrated *Ode (Intimations of Immortality from Recollections of Early Childhood):*

> *Our birth is but a sleep and a forgetting:*
> *The soul that rises with us, our life's star,*
> *Hath had elsewhere its setting,*
> *And cometh from afar:*
> *Not in entire forgetfulness,*
> *And not in utter nakedness,*
> *But trailing clouds of glory do we come*
> *From God who is our home.*
> *Heaven lies about us in our infancy!*

Another poet, Eliza R. Snow, reflected on this same theme in equally poetic words: "Ofttimes a secret something [whispers] 'You're a stranger here'—and we sense "that [we have] wandered from a more exalted sphere."[71]

And I have also been stirred, as I am sure many of you have, by Wordsworth's nostalgic description of the pleasures of his early childhood:

There was a time when meadow, grove, and stream,
The earth, and every common sight,
To me did seem
Appareled in celestial light,
The glory and the freshness of a dream.

But then Wordsworth sadly notes that this splendid vision often fades as we get caught up in the tasks of what we are wont to call adult life:

The youth, who daily farther from the east
Must travel, still is Nature's priest,
And by the vision splendid
Is on his way attended;
At length the man perceives it die away,
And fade into the light of common day.[72]

Wordsworth added to his lyrical reflections on life by saying:

O joy! that in our embers
Is something that doth live,
That nature yet remembers
What was so fugitive! . . .
The thought of our past years in me doth breed
Perpetual benediction.[73]

Beautiful language makes deep thoughts understandable and truly adds a wonderful dimension to life.

Creation: Consider also the beauties and the grandeur of nature. How often I have gazed with awe and wonder across the wide vistas of the desert, at the majesty of snow-capped mountains, the intimacy of seaside coves, the delicacy of a rosebud, or the engineering marvel of a spiderweb. In his joyful celebration of the greatness of the Lord, Stuart K. Hine penned these familiar words:

When thru the woods and forest glades I wander,
And hear the birds sing sweetly in the trees,
When I look down from lofty mountain grandeur
And hear the brook and feel the gentle breeze,
Then sings my soul, my Savior God, to thee,
How great thou art! How great thou art! [74]

Considering the beauties and wonders that give such pleasurable diversity to our world, it is easy for me to imagine that I did indeed shout for joy that I was to be sent by my Father to experience mortality in such a glorious setting.

The Senses: And, again, in my bag of gratitude, I cannot underestimate the splendid taste of a chocolate bar or an ice cream sundae, the fragrance of a flower, or the sounds of a child's voice or of a lovely piece of music. Have some of us become so jaded, so distracted by the challenges of life, that these remarkable, simple pleasures are overlooked or unappreciated?

Work: I am also grateful for daily labor. One of the conditions of mortality is that each must provide for himself by the sweat of his brow. If at times we may see this as a curse, it is less a curse than a glorious consequence of living. To labor, to exert our mind and body, to struggle both beside and with nature and our fellow-man, what possibilities lie therein! There are few things more satisfying than investing ourselves in a useful task and then successfully completing it. That is true of baking a cake, building a house, planting and harvesting a crop, or doing something more cerebral, such as writing a term paper or composing a piece of music. Unfortunate is the man or woman who has not discovered the joy of work.

Family and Friends: In my bag of gratitude are found those people with whom I have shared experiences and who have touched my life and made it sweet—both family members and friends. As a young assistant professor at the University of Virginia, I was laboring to write a manuscript in my office one beautiful autumn Saturday morning. There passed by my door an older colleague, who came in and inquired whether I had ever heard of a certain scholar. I admitted that I had not. He exclaimed, "Never heard of him?! A man who in the 1920s and 1930s was a leader in the field of political science and sociology, who had written hundreds of articles and scores of books, who was honored with innumerable awards for his work?!" I again confessed that I had never heard of him. To which my wise colleague responded, "Precisely! Go home, gather your family, and enjoy this fall day."

As the years roll by, I realize even more how precious are my wife, my children, my grandchildren, my extended family, my friends and colleagues, and many hundreds of Latter-day Saints. Let us rejoice in the love we have for our fellow travelers on this great journey through mortality.

Scriptures: Of all the riches of mortality, nothing gives greater joy, comfort, guidance, and peace than the dialogue between man and God. With Lehi, "My soul delighteth in the scriptures, and my heart pondereth them" (2 Nephi 4:15). With what raptures can the scriptures transport us! Scriptures are not simply the word of God, but they are the words of God as transmitted by mortal men, flesh and blood people with weaknesses and strengths, possibilities and limitations, like each of us. Nothing is so thrilling or reassuring as to see this interaction between man in mortality and immortal God. Each of us, as moved by the Holy Ghost, may for the profit of our family record our own interaction with the eternal within the daily bounds of mortal life. As Nephi noted, he recorded his own such experiences "for the learning and the profit of [his] children" (2 Nephi 4:15). If we have this vision and live in harmony with the Spirit, we may share the declarations and teachings of those who we call prophets, and we may, as Moses prayed, ourselves be prophets within our own stewardship (see Numbers 11:29).

Do you recall the movie that starred Robin Williams and Robert DeNiro, *The Awakening*? It was set in a hospital populated by individuals who through disease had lost their ability to relate to the world around them. Through persistence and experimentation, the physician was able to bring his patients back into reality. They were rescued from the prison imposed by encephalitis and were once again able to see and experience life. What exuberance and joy they demonstrated. How can we, then, reject or devalue such a life?

In the 59th section of the Doctrine and Covenants, the Lord explicitly condemns those who fail to show gratitude or to acknowledge His hand in their many blessings (see vv. 20–21). In another place, He promised: "And he who receiveth all things with thankfulness shall be made glorious; and the things of this earth shall be added unto him, even an hundred fold, yea, more" (D&C 78:19).

Repentance

After gratitude, we return again to repentance as a source of happiness. Ultimately, happiness depends on faith in Christ unto repentance. That faith implies that we not only believe that He is the Savior of Mankind, the Son of the Living God, but that we are prepared to trust in Him completely, to abandon our old self (yes, even the grouchy old self), and to yield to the promptings of the Holy Spirit so that we may have a new heart and a renewed mind. Repentance means, in the words of the prophets, a "mighty change of heart," a willingness to choose the right, an energetic effort to put things right, and a commitment to endure in keeping the right. In declaring that happiness is the object and design of our existence, the Prophet Joseph Smith added: "And [happiness] will be the end thereof, if we pursue the path that leads to it; and this path is virtue, uprightness, faithfulness, holiness, and keeping all the commandments of God."[75] Through the atonement of Christ, made operative in our lives through sacred covenants and ordinances, we will then triumph over the circumstances of our lives and achieve that peace that lies within—a peace which is at the core of happiness.

With the understanding and inner transformation born of such faith, we are prepared to act rather than simply react to the challenges of life. Indeed, the first fruits of such faith are charity and a forgiving heart. Not even the evils and ill will of others may then shatter us.

It is this understanding of the nature of life and this view of faith that are reflected in Christ's counsel to his apostles, "And fear not them which kill the body, but are not able to kill the soul: but rather fear him which is able to destroy both soul and body in hell. Are not two sparrows sold for a farthing? and one of them shall not fall on the ground without your Father. But the very hairs of your head are all numbered. Fear ye not therefore, ye are of more value than many sparrows" (Matthew 10:28–31).

On Not Looking Back

Once we have put our trust in Christ and with a broken heart and contrite spirit allowed the Holy Ghost to bring about the mighty change of our hearts and to renew our minds, it is incumbent on us not to look back to the old man or woman, the former habits and attitudes, the reprobate and bitter way of life.

Orpheus, the famous mythological Greek musician, was

reputed to be able through his music to control nature and charm wild animals. He:

> *Made the moveless trees to run,*
> *Made the rivers halt their flow,*
> *Made the lion, hind's fell foe*
> *Side by side with her to go,*
> *Made the hare accept the hound*
> *Subdued now by the music's sound.*

When his wife died, however, he himself could not be consoled. "Though his song all things subdued, it could not calm the master's mood." So, "down to [Hades, the world of the dead] he went for love."

His song subdued Cerberus, the mythical three-headed dog that guards the gates of the underworld; caused the vultures to suspend their grim task of tearing at the liver of the giant Tityus; soothed Tantalus, whose reach was always just short of the food or water he sought to reach; and elicited sympathy from the Furies, the mythological spirits of punishment.

At last Orpheus confronted the monarch of the dead, Pluto, who in tearful voice said, "We yield."

> *Let him take with him his wife,*
> *By song redeemed and brought to life.*
> *But let him too this law obey,*
> *Look not on her by the way*
> *Until from night she reaches day.*

But, alas, "close to bounds of night, Orpheus backward turned his sight and, looking, lost and killed her there."[76]

The moral drawn from this tale by the Roman philosopher Ancius Boethius (c. A.D. 475–525) is both poignant and timely:

> *Whoever seeks the upward way*
> *Lift your mind into the day;*
> *For who gives in and turns his eye*
> *Backward to darkness from the sky,*
> *Loses while he looks below*
> *All that up with him may go.*[77]

Recall the story of Lot and his wife as they fled Sodom and Gomorrah: The angels said to Lot, "Arise, take thy wife, and thy two daughters, which are here; lest thou be consumed in the iniquity of the city." But, they cautioned, "Look not behind thee."

Ignoring the warning, "his wife looked back from behind him, and she became a pillar of salt" (Genesis 19:15, 17, 26).

Harking back to Genesis and this incident, the mortal Messiah commented: "They did eat, they drank, they bought, they sold, they planted, they builded; But the same day that Lot went out of Sodom it rained fire and brimstone from heaven, and destroyed them all" (Luke 17:27–29).

In the day of commitment and of judgment, Jesus exhorted, let us not "return back." As He said, "Remember Lot's wife. Whosoever shall seek to save his life shall lose it; and whosoever shall lose his life shall preserve it" (vv. 31–33).

In the last day, as in the day of Lot, the neglectful, the wayward, and the inattentive will continue in their routine tasks and occupations as if they constituted the whole of life.

To succeed in our quest for eternal life, we must utterly break with the old life. Nostalgic backward glances and morbid reflections on the evil we may have abandoned will not save that life and will prevent us from obtaining eternal life.

The 30 December 1989 *Church News* recalls the story of "a man who watched a farmer plowing a field in preparation for planting a new crop. Later the spectator asked the farmer how he managed to plant such straight furrows. The farmer replied, 'I just fix my sight on a certain tree, bush, or fence post and then head straight for it.'"[78]

When I was the head of the Chief of Naval Operations' Strategic Studies Group, my colleagues and I compiled and inscribed "ten pretty good rules," of which one was, "Never look back unless you intend to go there."

Recall the plea of the psalmist: "Remember not the sins of my youth, nor my transgressions: according to thy mercy remember thou me for thy goodness' sake, O Lord" (Psalm 25:7).

To recall again, the Lord has promised in modern revelation: "Behold, he who has repented of his sins, the same is forgiven, and I, the Lord, remember them no more" (D&C 58:42).

How comforting is that?

Service

The final key, if joy is to abound, is performing Christ-like service, which is a fruit of faith and repentance and a manifestation of our hope. It is in making a consistent attempt to do good and to bless others that we are able to transcend the concerns of our own hearts. And as an incentive to practice this principle of happiness, the Lord has said, "For behold, it is not meet that I should command in all things; for he that is compelled in all things, the same is a slothful and not a wise servant; wherefore he receiveth no reward. Verily I say, men should be anxiously engaged in a good cause, and do many things of their own free will, and bring to pass much righteousness; For the power is in them, wherein they are agents unto themselves. And inasmuch as men do good they shall in nowise lose their reward" (D&C 58:26–28).

HOPE AND HAPPINESS: MAN IS THAT HE MIGHT HAVE JOY

Such gratitude, such repentance, such service keep hope bright even in the darkest hour. As Paul wrote, "And hope maketh not ashamed; because the love of God is shed abroad in our hearts by the Holy Ghost which is given unto us" (Romans 5:5). And again, "For we are saved by hope" (Romans 8:24). Hence, as Paul counseled, "Be not moved away from the hope of the gospel" (Colossians 1:23). Nephi's testimony is consistent with Paul's teachings: "Ye must press forward with a steadfastness in Christ, having a perfect brightness of hope, and a love of God and of all men. Wherefore, if ye shall press forward, feasting upon the word of Christ, and endure to the end, behold, thus saith the Father: Ye shall have eternal life" (2 Nephi 31:20).

Moroni, as have all the prophets, explains that the reward we shall receive in the final judgment will be the natural consequence of our behavior. He makes clear that through faith, repentance, service, and a grateful heart we may find happiness in this life, and that, having established the fundamentals of happiness now, joy will be ours eternally. There will be no miraculous transformation, for as Moroni explains: "And then cometh the judgment of the Holy One upon them; and then cometh the time that he that is filthy shall be filthy still; and he that is righteous shall be righteous still; he that is happy shall be happy still; and he that is unhappy shall be unhappy still" (Mormon 9:14).

May we cultivate the habits of happiness now so that happiness will be ours eternally.

PART THREE
TRUE DISCIPLESHIP

Edification and Daily Benevolence

In his great valedictory sermon to his people, King Benjamin exhorted, "I would that ye should take upon you the name of Christ, all you that have entered into the covenant with God that ye should be obedient unto the end of your lives" (Mosiah 5:8). Jesus Himself, during his mortal ministry, said to his followers, "If ye continue in my word, then are ye my disciples indeed" (John 8:31). Both the Lord and King Benjamin pointed to the defining characteristic of a disciple.

Disciple is related to the word *discipline.* Discipline denotes in the first instance a field of knowledge characterized by key questions, prescribed methods, and some fundamental answers. In the case of the gospel discipline, it points to *the* truth, that is, the fundamental doctrines and principles found in the word of God and exemplified by Christ. In effect, it refers us back to the notion of *true understanding.* But the Savior and Benjamin were signaling something more than simply understanding. Another aspect of a discipline is obedience to rules that correct, mold, and perfect the mental and moral faculties, in effect, shape *true character.* Finally, however, the sign of a *true disciple,* one who has undertaken the discipline of Christ, is that one is prepared to emulate in one's own life the example of the Master.

Christ explained to Thomas, when Thomas inquired as to the path that the Lord had prepared for his disciples, "I am the way, the truth, and the life" (John 14:5–6). In a real sense, the gospel is not simply a philosophy of life or a set of rules of conduct. It is a biography—the biography of Christ. He has invited us, as "partakers of the divine nature" (2 Peter 1:4), to participate in His biography, being with Him "joint heirs" of the glory of God (Romans 8:17). Hence, the resurrected Lord asked his Nephite disciples, "What manner of men ought ye to be?" And He answered, "Verily I say unto you, even as I am" (3 Nephi 27:27).

If we consider what manner of man Christ was and is, several facets of his personality stand out. First, He knew the truth and exemplified the truth; that is, He grasped and represented what the point of existence really is. As He declared to the Prophet Joseph Smith, "The Spirit of truth is of God. I am the Spirit of truth, and John bore record of me, saying: He received a fulness of truth, yea, even of all truth" (D&C 93:26).

Secondly, His Father was always with Him because He was obedient in all things. As he said, "And he that sent me is with me: the Father hath not left me alone; for I do always those things that please him" (John 8:29).

Third, Christ taught and exemplified love of God and man. Indeed, he saw such love as the sign of true discipleship: "By this shall all men know that ye are my disciples, if ye have love one to another" (John 13:35). This brotherly love was manifest in a unity of caring and purpose among His disciples. He enjoined them, "Bear ye one another's burdens, and so fulfil the law of Christ" (Galatians 6:2). He knew that such mutual concern and care of one another ultimately involves the sacrifice of all things we hold in preference to the kingdom of God and requires the consecration of our time, talents, and resources to bear up others and to establish on earth the kingdom of His Father.

Hence, he said to the good young man who inquired how to obtain eternal life, "If thou wilt be perfect, go and sell that thou has, and give to the poor, and thou shalt have treasure in heaven: and come and follow me" (Matthew 19:21). This final price of discipleship was more, however, than the young man could give, for it is written, "He went away sorrowful; for he had great possessions" (v. 19:22).

While I was serving as a missionary in France, the London Temple was completed, only the second temple in Europe. All the missionaries in the French missions were given permission to cross the English Channel and participate in the dedication of the temple. We all, however, needed to be interviewed in order to receive a recommend to attend the dedication. As it transpired, all of us were interviewed by a General Authority, in my case by Elder Richard L. Evans of the Quorum of the Twelve Apostles. I shall never forget that interview.

Elder Evans simply asked me two questions. The first was: "Elder Wood, are you prepared to give up your life in defense of the witness of Christ and His restored gospel?" Being young and totally incapable of hallucinating my own death, I answered much too readily and cavalierly, "Sure!" But then he asked a question that I knew was an "IOU" that was immediately and forever due: "Elder Wood, are you willing to give up all you have and all you are, all that you shall ever have or be, to bring forth and establish the cause of Zion?" After a pause and with greater humility, I answered, "Yes."

Over the years, although I always remembered the interview,

I did not think too much about the commitment I had made. Then, in the spring of 1999, my wife and I were taking a little inventory of how satisfactory everything was in our life. We noted how much I enjoyed my work and that I had no real intentions of ever retiring. I was also enjoying my Church calling, as was my wife hers. We had four wonderful daughters and marvelous grandchildren, all considerably above average! Some of the grandchildren lived just down the street from us, so we were able to spend time with them on a regular basis. And above all things, the cat and dog had died! Now, you may ask, why this was so important. Well, it meant we could get a new carpet and, with a new carpet, we also remodeled the kitchen and had two of the bedrooms redone, one into a study and another into a workroom for my wife. With the dog gone, it was also probably time to consider redoing the lawn. And, most important, from my wife's perspective, I had committed to getting central air conditioning. I had always resisted such importuning with the standard answer given in New England, "Oh, you don't need air conditioning in New England. It isn't hot and humid that long." Well, of course, this is self-delusional, for often it is hot and humid for a very long time. In any case, I said, "Okay, let's do it." Everything seemed very satisfactory and completely under control. And then the telephone rang.

It was President Gordon B. Hinckley, and he called us to give it all up—to put aside the house, my job, the comfortable life, and to assist in other ways to bring forth and establish the cause of Zion. As he spoke, the words of Richard L. Evans came back to me and, indeed, even the words of the Savior to the young man. This also was part of discipleship. Although it is true, as it always proves to be, that the rewards of responding to the call have been glorious, the crucial element of discipleship is the willingness to follow, the willingness to make whatever sacrifices may be required, and the willingness to consecrate everything to the Lord's work. As the Lord and his prophets beckon, whether it is to some distant land or to a change in the course of our daily lives, we are asked to give. This "giving" always in some way entails blessing others, edifying them, and thereby building the kingdom of God on the earth—bringing forth and establishing the cause of Zion.

In the next two chapters, we will consider various dimensions of discipleship—how through word and deed we bear one another's burdens, lift others, strengthen our families and communities, and establish the Lord's kingdom. To be a disciple is to willingly and happily follow the admonition of Paul to edify one another. For as the Savior taught, "Inasmuch as ye have done it unto one of the least of these my brethren, ye have done it unto me" (Matthew 25:40).

CHAPTER 5

Things Wherewith One May Edify Another

As he invited those who had responded to his preaching to enter the waters of baptism, Alma declared the conditions of that covenant to be both personal and communal. Each convert covenants to serve God, to keep His commandments, and to stand as a witness of God at all times and in all places. At the same time, the individual being baptized covenants to enter into a community of Saints, bearing one another's burdens that they may be light, comforting one another, and mourning with those that mourn (see Mosiah 18:8–10).

In His visit to the Book of Mormon lands, the resurrected Lord commissioned the twelve disciples to preach His gospel unto all people upon the face of the land that they might be "converted unto the Lord, and [be] united unto the church of Christ," that they all might be blessed (3 Nephi 28:23). Conversion to Christ is thus linked to union with His church.

Speaking of that church, Moroni wrote that all those so linked should "be remembered and nourished by the good word of God, to keep them in the right way, to keep them continually watchful unto prayer, relying alone upon the merits of Christ, who was the author and the finisher of their faith." To achieve these things, the Saints met together often, fasting and praying, renewing their covenants, and speaking "one with another concerning the welfare of their souls" (Moroni 6:4–6).

In the ancient Mediterranean church, the apostles expressed their ongoing concerns for the spiritual and temporal welfare of the Saints. The book of the Acts of the Apostles and also the New Testament epistles are filled with counsel encouraging the members to sustain each other in their faith and in their trials. The word often used in scripture for this mutual support, this building up of one another, is *edification.*

The Apostle Paul counseled the Saints, "Let us therefore follow after the things which make for peace, and things wherewith one may edify another" (Romans 14:19). He noted that the gifts of God are given to benefit all, and he counseled the Romans, "We then that are strong ought to bear the infirmities of the weak, and not to please ourselves" (Romans 15:1). To the Saints at Corinth, Paul sent a direct but gentle chiding, advising the spiritually zealous: "Forasmuch as ye are zealous of spiritual gifts, seek that ye may excel to the edifying of the church" (1 Corinthians 14:12).

In his epistle to the Ephesians, Paul compared the Church to the body of Christ and summarized its purposes, which are: "for the perfecting of the saints, for the work of the ministry, for the edifying of the body of Christ." Moreover, the Church is to continue its work: "Till we all come in the unity of the faith, and of the knowledge of the Son of God, unto a perfect man, unto the measure of the stature of the fulness of Christ" (Ephesians 4:12–13; see also verses 14–16).

The apostles and prophets have drawn our attention to the

two sides of the saintly coin: first, each of us is called out of the world in faith unto repentance to stand as "witnesses of God at all times and in all things, and in all places"; second, we are invited into a communion dedicated to mutual edification. And as the Church succeeds it becomes a beacon to the world, drawing to it those who seek righteousness. The work of the Lord initially prospered in those former days, to the extent that the apostles reported: "Then had the churches rest throughout all Judea and Galilee and Samaria, and were edified; and walking in the fear of the Lord, and in the comfort of the Holy Ghost, were multiplied" (Acts 9:31).

THE WAYS OF DIMINISHMENT

As the dark clouds of the apostasy began to enfold the Church, the counsel of the shepherds to whom Christ had entrusted leadership was ignored. One can see in the epistles to the branches of the Church a growing alarm that the work of edification was threatened by forces that would disunite and diminish. Finally, by the second century after the birth of Christ, if the form of godliness remained, the power thereof had been lost, and a dark age began to descend, from whose gloom only the power of heaven could rescue.

To understand edification more clearly, it may be well to consider its antithesis, diminishment. Let us consider three ways diminishment manifests itself in the Church and explore how, consciously or unconsciously, we ourselves might contribute to it.

Diminishment might be seen, first, in dwindling belief; second, in a tendency for Saints to demean and belittle one another; and third, in active disobedience.

Dwindling Belief

The Lord warned Nephi of the dangers of a nation dwindling and perishing in unbelief, a theme to which Nephi returned again and again. To dwindle is to waste away. Contrary to the word of God swelling within us and increasing our stature, dwindling in unbelief is an implosion into a black hole in which the hope of the gospel perishes. Too often, I fear, we heal not the unbelief of our brothers and sisters, but we fuel it. On the one hand, through our own limited perspective, or at times even an invincible ignorance on our own part, we add to the fears and doubts of those whose testimonies are weak. We seek not to understand and to follow the counsels of the prophets, we ponder not the scriptures, and we depart from an attitude of fasting and prayer. In the midst of this confusion, we reinforce the doubts and fears of others.

In addition, there are times when the gap between our profession of faith and our behavior is so wide that it breeds cynicism in those who observe us. This is particularly harmful to those who have barely begun to imbibe the milk of the gospel and have not yet advanced to the meat that will build spiritual muscle. It is not only our own failure to understand that weakens others but also our hypocrisy.

On the other hand, we often feel that we are building the faith of our brothers and sisters by correcting their misunderstanding of gospel truths. While correction may be required, the task of doing so should be approached with fear and trembling. Some of us have a particular stewardship to maintain the integrity of the faith. All of us should defend truth and righteousness. But whether we seek to correct error as a duty of the office we hold or out of concern for our fellow citizen in the kingdom of God, remember this: no effective correction is possible without the exercise of patience, long-suffering, and love. As Paul observed, "Knowledge puffeth up, but charity edifieth" (1 Corinthians 8:1).

Demeaning Behavior

A second cause of diminishment is demeaning behavior. There are three tools of derision that are especially damaging in human relations: mockery, cynicism, and sarcasm.

Mockery is to treat with scorn or contempt; to deride; to ridicule; to mimic in sport; to scoff, or to jeer. It constitutes an attempt to demoralize or demean so as to bring others or their ideas into contempt. Mockery is a primary tool of those who occupy the large and spacious building that father Lehi saw in vision. At the day of Pentecost, some were amazed and marveled while others mocked, saying the believers were drunk with new wine. Jude, the brother of Christ, warned that "there should be mockers in the last time, who should walk after their own ungodly lusts, These be they who separate themselves, sensual, not having the Spirit" (Jude 1:17–19). And during His final passion, in an act of monumental ignorance, the mindless mob cruelly mocked Him who would be their Savior.

Mockery is a behavior that must be eschewed by a disciple of Christ.

Closely related to mockery is the spirit of cynicism and the use of sarcasm. Cynics are disposed to find and to catch at fault. Implicitly or explicitly, they display a sneering disbelief in sincerity and rectitude. Isaiah described those who "watch for iniquity" and "make a man an offender for a word, and lay a snare for him that reproveth in the gate, and turn aside the just for a thing of nought" (Isaiah 29:20–21). In this dispensation, the Lord has commanded that we "cease to find fault one with another" and "above all things, clothe [ourselves] with the bond of charity, as with a mantle, which is the bond of perfectness and peace" (D&C 88:124, 125).

Mockers and cynics are seldom courageous but often cover their attacks in language that allows them to feign injured innocence if challenged. Such language is called sarcasm—the use of bitter, caustic, scoffing, or stinging remarks, expressing contempt, often by ironical statements.

Unfortunately, the spirit of mockery, cynicism, and sarcasm is found not only in the world but is carried into our congregations and our homes. The effects of such a spirit are to generate contention, give offense, desensitize feelings, demoralize many, and to drive the Holy Ghost from our midst.

Such activity not only demeans others and attacks the very integrity of the community, but it also diminishes those who engage in it. As it says in Proverbs 14:6, "A scorner seeketh wisdom, and findeth it not." Francis Bacon (1561–1626), following this theme, wrote: "He that cometh to seek after knowledge with a mind to scorn and censure shall be sure to find matter for his humor, but none for his instruction."[79] Henry Ward Beecher (1812–1887) perhaps put most succinctly the deprivation and the depravation of the cynic: "The cynic is one who never sees a good quality in a man, and never fails to see a bad one—He is the human owl, vigilant in darkness and blind to light, mousing for vermin and never seeing noble game."[80] Alma sounded this warning for those members of the Church who by their scorn and cynical sneering become a stumbling block for their brethren and sisters: "And again I say unto you, is there one among you that doth make a mock of his brother, or that heapeth upon him persecutions? Wo unto such an one" (Alma 5:30–31).

As Alma stated, such cynical, mocking, sarcastic behavior not only diminishes ourselves but can also destroy others. Returning to Lehi's vision, you recall that many who had followed the word of God to the tree of life, had experienced the love of God and had embarked on the road to eternal life, but later had fallen away due to the mockery of those who were of the worldly mind.

C. S. Lewis once said that all of us are of divine parentage and heirs to eternal glory, in a real sense potential gods and goddesses, and we in our relations with each other either advance others toward this goal or toward the opposite extreme.[81] This is perhaps why Thomas Carlyle (1795–1881) said that "Sarcasm is the language of the devil."[82] Of those who cause their brother and sister to stumble through mockery, cynicism, and sarcasm—or any other diminishing word or act, the Lord has said, "And calamity shall cover the mocker, and the scorner shall be consumed; and they that have watched for iniquity shall be hewn down and cast into the fire" (D&C 45:50). Within the body of Christ, let us edify one another. Let it not be said that we have failed to heed Jacob's warning: "Will ye . . . quench the Holy Spirit, and make a mock of the grand plan of redemption?" (Jacob 6:8).

Disobedience

The third and final cause of diminishment that I would signal is converting our associations within the body of Christ into a community of disobedience. Man is a social being. In all his doing, he craves association and fellowship and seeks a community to legitimize his thoughts and acts. There are not only communities of Saints but bands of robbers. Again I am struck in reading the apostolic epistles, as well as the writings of the Book of Mormon and the sermons of latter-day prophets, how within the body of Christ cliques and bands can grow. They seek special exemption from the Lord's commandments and the direction of the prophets. They make one aspect of the gospel into a hobby and confuse the part with the whole. They claim superior insight into the mind and will of God. They divide the body of Christ.

THE WAYS OF EDIFICATION

Leaving that which diminishes, let us turn to that which edifies. Among the contributors to edification, I would note five. First, the work of edification is directed by the Spirit. President Joseph Fielding Smith wrote that "all light, all truth come from God. That which is not from him does not edify but brings darkness."[83] Second, edification is closely connected to charity, the pure love of Christ, and "charity edifieth" (1 Corinthians 8:1). Third, edification is fostered by a unity of righteous purpose and effort. "If ye are not one," said the Lord, "ye are not mine" (D&C 38:27). Fourth, edification is affirmed and demonstrated in good works. The Apostle James defines the life of a Saint as "pure religion," which is shown forth not in grand sermons but in a listening ear, a receptive heart, and a willing hand. We are to be doers of the word, not hearers only. Representative of pure religion is to "visit the fatherless and widows in their affliction, and to keep [oneself] unspotted from the world." In bearing one another's burden that they may be light, we shall sow in peace (see James 1:27; 3:18). Fifth and finally, edification is shaped by "holy communication." We communicate one with another in words, music, gestures, and appearances. It is important that we also evaluate these activities from the point of view of whether they invite all to come to and be perfected in Christ.

Of these five, let us consider just one in some detail—the issue of "holy communication" and its opposite, "corrupt communication." In the matter of edification, the apostles and prophets have lavished enormous attention on the issue of how we communicate.

Holy Communication

Consider the importance of our language. Both philosophers and prophets have asserted that who we are and what we say are intimately related. Not only is man distinguished in his humanity by speech, but he is moved to acts—good and evil—by what he and others utter. Christ taught that our words reveal us; our words shape us; and our words influence, directly and indirectly, the souls of others—how they see themselves and what they do.

Jesus declared that we will be judged by what comes out of our mouths—our words, our utterances, our blessings, our curses. The type of person we are and shall become is largely shaped by our thoughts, which in turn is reflected in our speech, which further shapes what we are becoming. If we speak the words of the gutter, we shall inherit the gutter; if we utter words of anger and hate, we shall become rage itself; if we speak carnally, we shall die as to our spiritual nature; if we curse Deity, we shall become a curse.

Alternatively, if we have taken upon us the name of Jesus Christ and undertake to walk in His path, allowing the baptism of fire and the Holy Ghost to purge us of all filth, we shall be heir to the promise expressed by Nephi: "After ye have entered in by the way . . . and received the Holy Ghost ye [shall] speak with the tongue of angels" (2 Nephi 32:1–2). Christ shall be in us and we in Christ so that we become united with him as heirs and coheirs of the glory of God.

Christ described most explicitly and most soberingly how our words reveal us:

A good man out of the good treasure of the heart bringeth forth good things: and an evil man out of the evil treasure bringeth forth evil things. But I say unto you, That every idle word that men shall speak, they shall give account thereof in the day of judgment. For by thy words thou shalt be justified, and by thy words thou shalt be condemned. [Matthew 12:35–37]

Our words not only *reveal* our inner being but also *shape* it. Christ emphasized: "Not that which goeth into the mouth defileth a man; but that which cometh out of the mouth, this defileth a man" (Matthew 15:11).

The Apostle Paul wrote, "Be not deceived" [that is, don't kid yourself, pay attention to this, it matters!]: evil communications [for example, bad words, obscene language, swearing, gossip, angry outbursts] corrupt good manners [ruin good character]" (1 Corinthians 15:33). Therefore, "Let all bitterness, and wrath, and anger, and clamour, and evil speaking, be put away from you, with all malice: And be ye kind one to another, even as God for Christ's sake hath forgiven you" (Ephesians 4:31–32).

Let us be sure we fully grasp what Paul is saying: When we take the name of God in vain as a curse or exclamation; when we trivialize, degrade, or make mockery of the sacred power of pro-creation, sex; when we speak with irreverence or vulgarity—what the Lord calls "light-mindedness" and "loud laughter"; when we demean with mockery and sarcasm; when we rage intemperately; when we do these things, the Holy Spirit departs and the spirit of Satan enters in, corrupting us and perhaps those around us.

The exhortation of the Lord recorded in the 88th section of Doctrine and Covenants, called by the Prophet Joseph Smith the "olive leaf," is worth noting in this context: "Cease from all your light speeches, from all laughter, from all your lustful desires, from all your pride and light-mindedness, and from all your wicked doings" (v. 121). This exhortation is not trivial. It says that our demeanor—appearance, language, gestures, behavior—is related to our sanctification—becoming like Christ and therefore like our true selves. This "external observance" has thus been associated with what is called the "Law of the Gospel."

Doctrine and Covenants 88 is a remarkable and profound analysis by the Lord of the way of sanctification and the final fate of the world. It links our demeanor (external observances) and our mutual edification ("All may be edified of all"—D&C 88:122) to this sanctification—that is, Christ is revealed in us, and we with Him are united to the Father.

The idea that we should so speak and act that "all may be edified of all" affirms the understanding that our words mold others and establish our relationship to them. It is interesting that the Apostle John used the analogy of the **Word** of God to describe Christ. Christ revealed the Father—Christ is, in a manner of speaking, God's utterance—and, through the expression of His life, He established His identity with the Father and invited us to join in this unity. (See Romans 8:14, 16; 9:26. Also Galatians 3:28; John 1:12; 2 Corinthians 6:18; Mosiah 5:7, 15; 27:25.)

By our utterances, then, the words we make manifest, we also invite others to a certain kind of life and a certain set of relationships. The special responsibility given by the Lord to holders of the Aaronic Priesthood in the matter of our "demeanor" has applicability to all of us, for the members of that priesthood are exhorted to "watch over the church" to see that "there is no iniquity in the church, neither hardness with each other, neither lying, backbiting, nor evil speaking" (D&C 20:53–54).

Speech, and its edifying power, is not confined only to words but is also expressed in rhythms, harmony, and pitch—in music.

Elder Bruce R. McConkie once remarked, "Music is part of the language of the Gods."[84]

The comfort, the strength, the edification that music can provide in our lives has been brought home to me as I have contemplated the atoning sacrifice. The great trial Christ endured in Gethsemane and on Calgary was prefaced by music: "And when they had sung an hymn, they went out into the mount of Olives" (Matthew 26:30).

The power of music to shape and to motivate, to purge and to sanctify, to teach and to ennoble is almost beyond comprehension. The majestic strains of Handel's *Messiah* transport us back to that holy night of Jesus' birth when "suddenly there was with the angel a multitude of the heavenly host praising God, and saying, Glory to God in the highest, and on earth peace, good will toward men" (Luke 2:13–14).

The singing by John Taylor of "A Poor Wayfaring Man of Grief" served as a backdrop to that awful moment when, the forces of darkness gathering and the jaws of hell gaping, violent men murdered the Prophet of the Restoration. Joseph sealed his testimony with his blood and with the strains of that tender hymn echoing in his ears.

While singing "The Spirit of God like a fire is burning" in the Kirtland Ohio Stake conference several years ago, I was transported in my mind to the Kirtland Temple, once again bathed in light, and my ears could almost hear the voice of Jehovah solemnly proclaiming: "The fame of this house shall spread to foreign lands; and this is the beginning of the blessing which shall be poured out upon the heads of my people" (D&C 110:10).

Through music, the boy David calmed the troubled spirit of King Saul: "And it came to pass, when the evil spirit, which was not of God, was upon Saul, that David took a harp, and played with his hand; so Saul was refreshed, and was well, and the evil spirit departed from him" (JST 1 Samuel 16:23).

It is not surprising that one of the first revelations given after the organization of the Church was the charge given to Emma Smith:

> And it shall be given thee, also, to make a selection of sacred hymns, as it shall be given thee, which is pleasing unto me, to be had in my church. *For my soul delighteth in the song of the heart; yea, the song of the righteous is a prayer unto me, and it shall be answered with a blessing upon their heads.* [D&C 25:11–12; emphasis added]

Elder Boyd K. Packer, Acting President of the Quorum of the Twelve Apostles, tells the story of his preparing to address newly called mission presidents and regional representatives in the Assembly Hall on Temple Square. He was to deliver what, in my opinion, was one of the most magnificent sermons of this dispensation, wherein he called those in attendance to recover the spirit of "Box B."[85] Box B was once the return mailing address of the First Presidency. When one received a letter from that box, as did the father of young Ezra Taft Benson, to depart immediately on a mission, the recipient left the plow in the field, set aside immediate cares, and answered the Lord's call—an act similar to that of the fishermen of Galilee.

In spite of the nobility of sentiments and the inspiration of the counsel, Elder Packer felt something additional was needed. He conferred with his wife, who suggested that there be sung an old Primary song, fallen into disuse. She and Elder Packer went to the piano and sang together the forgotten hymn. He knew that this was to be the great instrument of edification. On the evening of his presentation, elders and sisters from the MTC in Provo were waiting in the basement of the Assembly Hall for the final moments of Elder Packer's instruction. On a signal, they filed up the stairs and marched down the aisles of the Assembly Hall to the front of the chapel, singing in unison. Under the inspiration of that "sweet compulsion" all in the audience arose as one, tears streaming down their faces, hearts racing, and spirits soaring. That stirring melody along with the inspiring words of the song gave dramatic confirmation to the charge of Elder Packer: "Called to Serve."

Surely John Milton spoke the truth, "Sweet compulsion doth in music lie."[86]

Just as words may help us edify one another, musical expression may do likewise. We may be edified together by our language and by our music, or we may be diminished if our words and our song betray the false spirits. As the Lord has said in this dispensation: "Behold, verily I say unto you, that there are many spirits which are false spirits, which have gone forth in the earth, deceiving the world. And also Satan hath sought to deceive you, that he might overthrow you" (D&C 50:2–3).

As to whether or not something is edifying, Moroni has given us this standard: "I show unto you the way to judge; for every thing which inviteth to do good, and to persuade to believe in Christ, is sent forth by the power and gift of Christ; wherefore ye may know with a perfect knowledge it is of God. But whatsoever thing persuadeth men to do evil, and believe not in Christ, and deny him, and serve not God, then ye may know with a perfect knowledge it is of the devil" (Moroni 7:16–17).

Divine Influence and Meekness

What is the sum of the whole matter of edification? To build each other in Christ, we must seek to live and act as Christ would.

Divine influence and saintly authority are Christ-centered and reflective of divine principles. Worldly authority seeks to cover sins or to gratify vain ambitions. It betrays a spirit of pride and self-gratification. It aims at "unrighteous dominion" and often seeks to "counsel the Lord." It also influences through flattery, falsehood and half-truth, and compulsion (See D&C 121).

That which edifies in Christ is characterized by persuasion, long-suffering, gentleness and meekness, love unfeigned, kindness, and virtuous thought. These virtues comprise "meekness," which was the essence of the Savior's ministry. Meekness is compatible with strength and indeed may be strength's precondition. It includes having an openness to the inspiration of heaven. Indeed, to those who are meek, it is promised that "pure knowledge" will be imparted, that is, the inspiration of the Holy Ghost, which knowledge leads not to arrogance but an enlarged soul full of wisdom (see again D&C 121). We should also remember that the Lord promised the meek that they will inherit the earth (see Matthew 5:5).

Meekness is the defining characteristic of Christ: "Learn of me, for I am meek," he declared (Matthew 11:29). Paul counseled the Saints to "put on meekness" (Colossians 3:12), and James associated it with wisdom (see James 3:13–18). Moroni declared that none are acceptable before God, except the meek (see Moroni 7:44). Finally, the Lord declared in this dispensation that we are edified in meekness and that the priesthood may only be exercised in meekness (see D&C 84:106; 121:41).

As we build one another, let us remember, therefore, in the words of the resurrected Lord, "He that speaketh, whose spirit is contrite, whose language is meek and edifieth, the same is of God if he obey mine ordinances. . . . And if any man among you be strong in the Spirit, let him take with him that is weak, that he may be edified in all meekness, that he may become strong also" (D&C 52:16; 84:106). As we edify one another in meekness, we shall be bathed in light, and we shall live in a perpetual Sabbath.

CHAPTER 6

The Necessary Labors of the Day
and a Mighty Change of Heart

On the evening of 21 September 1823, Joseph Smith was contemplating his own weaknesses and the persecution he had suffered as a result of his testimony of the visitation of the Father and Son in the spring of 1820. He supplicated God that he might better understand his situation. While so engaged in prayer, a light appeared in the room which, as he later wrote, "continued to increase until the room was lighter than at noonday," in the midst of which appeared a personage who announced himself to be "a messenger sent from the presence of God . . . , and that his name was Moroni" (Joseph Smith–History 1:29–32).

Thus began the work that would bring forth the Book of Mormon as another witness of Christ and culminate in the restoration of the priesthood and the establishment of the restored Church.

Three times throughout the night Moroni appeared, explaining the foundations of this great and marvelous work and rehearsing the words of the ancient prophets as they had looked forward to this day. These events occupied the entire night, and upon the completion of the third visit, Joseph Smith, physically and probably emotionally exhausted, heard the cock crow. What then? He wrote, "I shortly after arose from my bed, and, as usual, went to the necessary labors of the day" (vv. 47–48).

I am struck by this matter-of-fact engagement in the ordinary business of life. On the day following one of the great divine manifestations in history, large with the fate of mankind and preparatory to the second coming of the Savior, Joseph Smith, "as usual," took up the "necessary labors of the day." In all the momentous events of his life, this pattern persisted.

As Saints of the latter days, all of us may be engaged in labors to bring forth Zion and establish the Kingdom of God. It may well be that we shall engage in heroic efforts comparable to the great revelatory events in Kirtland, the struggles in Missouri and Illinois, the epic pioneer trek across the Great Plains. But I would venture that our lives—who we are and what we are becoming—will largely be defined by our going about the necessary and usual labors of the day—getting up and going to work, tending the children, driving teenagers to Saturday activities, doing schoolwork, shoveling snow from our neighbor's driveway, doing home and visiting teaching, instructing in Primary, and singing in the ward choir.

Whether we are Relief Society president or Sunday School secretary, bishop or assistant librarian, when we are weighed in the divine balance, it will not be by reference to our résumé or curriculum vitae, but in response to the simple question: "Who really are you?" If the final judgment were to be a courtroom trial, would it be our defense attorney or the prosecutor who would call up as witnesses our spouse, our children, our employers, our employees, our fellow workers, our teachers, our classmates, the paperboy or girl, the store clerk, and/or our next door neighbor?

Sir Philip Sidney, the sixteenth-century English soldier and poet, observed, "A noble heart, like the sun, showeth its greatest countenance in its lowest estate."[87] What are we showing forth in our "lowest estate," that is, in the ordinary business of living? You may recall in Dante's *Divine Comedy* that he peopled the more fearful portions of purgatory and the lower reaches of hell with some notable characters, including several bishops of Rome. On the other hand, in the highest reaches of heaven were found some remarkably undistinguished and obscure souls. The difference being that those who achieved divine distinction did so, not by their mortal positions of influence or even ecclesiastical responsibilities, but by the charity, benevolence, good humor, and endurance exhibited in the normal labors of the day. We must show forth grace in our priesthood and Church callings, but we should also demonstrate that grace even in the "lowest estate" of living.

As mentioned in the introductory chapter, in a much-praised study entitled *The Face of Battle,* John Keegan examines the drama of war, not in terms of the great issues that provoke and may be decided by battle, but from the point of view of the common soldier who is in the thick of it. From that vantage point, the real qualities of each man may be more certainly assessed. Not the grand strategies, the military plans, the sweep of the campaigns, but the exertions of each individual as he stands on his little plot. I would suggest that the Master had this broad face of battle in mind when he said:

> And before him shall be gathered all nations: and he shall separate them one from another, as a shepherd divideth his sheep from the goats: And he shall set the sheep on his right hand, but the goats on the left. Then shall the King say unto them on his right hand, Come, ye

blessed of my Father, inherit the kingdom prepared for you from the foundation of the world: For I was an hungered, and ye gave me meat: I was thirsty, and ye gave me drink: I was a stranger, and ye took me in: Naked, and ye clothed me: I was sick, and ye visited me: I was in prison, and ye came unto me. Then shall the righteous answer him, saying, Lord, when saw we thee an hungered, and fed thee? or thirsty, and gave thee drink? When saw we thee a stranger, and took thee in? or naked, and clothed thee? Or when saw we thee sick, or in prison, and came unto thee? And the King shall answer and say unto them, Verily I say unto you, Inasmuch as ye have done it unto one of the least of these my brethren, ye have done it unto me. [Matthew 25:32–40]

It is in the thick of everyday living and the charity exhibited therein that we encounter the Christ.

Heroism in the Labors of the Day

Over the years I have been blessed to meet and be edified by many individuals who have exhibited the grace of God and the countenance of the Master. These men and women loom before me as heroic figures. They were in all stations of life, many neither prominent in the affairs of the world nor in the administration of the affairs of the Church.

As a bishop in Virginia, I came to know a man and woman, born in humble circumstances and possessing little formal education. They had nine children, and the husband worked for meager compensation in a local dairy. There was no hot water and no central heating in their home, only a wood-burning stove in the living room. They owned an unreliable automobile, one of Henry Ford's originals I would guess. They had no vacations and strayed not far from the environs of Albemarle County.

Once, when I was soliciting financial assistance for the Boy Scouts, the father came up to me and pressed a $20.00 bill in my hand. It might as well have been $20,000 for most other people. Despite my protests, he insisted that I take the money, saying, "I have boys in Scouting, and I must do my part." And do their part that family did. In Church assignments and in the divine stewardship of parenthood, their sun shone forth in the "lowest estate." Their children all took music lessons, all were assisted every night with homework, and all were prepared for the temple and a mission.

Today those children serve as members of elders quorum presidencies, as bishops, as Primary teachers, as counselors in Relief Societies, as prominent and successful members of their professions, and as outstanding parents. Each went on a mission, each has been sealed in the temple, and each received an advanced degree. Over the years, through hard labor and frugal management, this couple improved their material circumstances, but in the everyday circumstances of their lives, they "as usual," persisted in the "necessary labor of the day."

I have a close friend, a talented academic, once staff director of an important congressional committee, a former bishop, stake president, and mission president. He often talked when we were both students about how fearful he was of having a Down's syndrome child or one similarly limited. As it turned out, his last child, a son, has Down's syndrome. In the days that followed that son's birth, the true nobility of this man and his wife shone forth. I have stayed in their home. I have seen a family united in love and committed to doing all in their power for this child. This child knows he is loved. In all the fame and accomplishments of this man, it is in his devotion to the necessary labors of the day that I have seen the face of God.

I have seen families struggling with unemployment or underemployment while holding their children close to them and continuing to serve others. Living on food storage and scrimping to stay afloat, afflicted with deaths or illnesses in their broader family, and yet maintaining their sense of humor, they have continued in a life of service and their vibrant testimonies. I have been touched simply by what we are wont to call ordinary people going about ordinary tasks with extraordinary grace.

In my opinion, these are heroic figures. They are they who shall "overcome by faith, and [be] sealed by the Holy Spirit of promise . . . into whose hands the Father [will give] all things" (D&C 76:53, 55). In the midst of the necessary labors of the day, they have undergone the "mighty change of heart," being transformed into the image of Christ. It is of these that the Master will say, "Ye have done it unto me," and who, as the Apostle John said, shall see Christ, for they shall be like Him (see 1 John 3:3).

A MIGHTY CHANGE OF HEART

What exactly is the source of the heroic grace these wonderful individuals have demonstrated? What is the "mighty change of heart" that has enabled them to rise above all things?

Alma asked the members of the Church in Zarahemla to remember how God had delivered their fathers from the tyranny of King Noah and the bondage of the Lamanites. But, more important than this deliverance, he reminded them, was the change the Lord had wrought in their hearts (see Alma 5:7). He asked his listeners if they, too, had "experienced this mighty change in [their] hearts." Was there, he inquired, engraved upon their countenance the image of God? (see Alma 5:19).

Since ancient times, the image of the heart refers to the innermost soul, the fundamental character of the individual. Francis Bacon (1561–1626) thus observed, "All our actions take their hue from the complexion of the heart, as landscapes their variety from light."[88] And the great English orator, Earl Philip Chesterfield (1694–1773), grasped that the fundamental disposition of the soul affects even our understanding. As he wrote to his son, " . . . the heart governs the understanding."[89] Who we are in our innermost being determines what we perceive, what we think, what we hear, and what we say.

The prophets have always been discomfited by the fact that though the glory of God is visible everywhere, men and women oft "have eyes, and see not, [and] have ears, and hear not" (Jeremiah 5:21; see also Ezekiel 12:2; Isaiah 43:8). The Lord sets watchmen over His people and invites them: "Harken to the sound of the trumpet!" But the rebellious people respond, "We will not harken" (Jeremiah 6:17). To which the Lord replies, "My people are destroyed for lack of knowledge" (Hosea 4:6). This stubborn and rebellious spirit, this hardness of heart, can only be healed if the people are humbled even to the breaking of their hearts. Anything less than this is insufficient to get their attention.

It is this obdurate fact that the English novelist Edward George Bulwer-Lytton (1803–73) had in mind when he wrote, "The depraved and sinful heart does not of itself grow better, but goes on from bad to worse; but the heart renewed by divine grace grows steadily in the divine likeness; its path is that of the just, that shineth more and more to the perfect day."[90] And, as Chesterfield added, "It is much easier to pull up many weeds out of a garden, than one corruption out of the heart; to procure a hundred flowers to adorn a knot, than one grace to beautify the soul. The heart never grows better [simply] by age; I fear rather worse, always harder; a young liar will be an old one and a young knave will only be a greater knave as he grows older."[91]

The transformation of the soul, the heart of man, has been portrayed by prophets, ancient and modern, as arising from faith in the Lord and repentance and as being realized by an act of divine grace. One must first humble oneself in contrition at one's sins and shortcomings; one must be prepared to break the heart. As the psalmist wrote, "A broken spirit and a contrite heart, O God, thou wilt not despise" (Psalm 51:17). Again, the psalmist cries out, "Create in me a clean heart, O God; and renew a right spirit within me" (Psalm 51:10). Rudyard Kipling, in his great recessional in celebration of the power of the British Empire, reminds the people of the attribute that is ultimately required of them:

Still stands thine ancient sacrifice
An humble and a contrite heart.[92]

Under these conditions, the magnificent power of grace is revealed; the individual is reconciled with his better self; and his self, so sanctified, is reconciled to God. This, along with the Resurrection, is the essence of the Atonement.

To an individual and a people so prepared, the Lord declares:

A new heart also will I give you, and a new spirit will I put within you: and I will take away the stony heart out of your flesh, and I will give you an heart of flesh. And I will put my spirit within you, and cause you to walk in my statutes, and ye shall keep my judgments, and do them. [Ezekiel 36:26–27]

Dr. Terrance D. Olson, professor in The School of Family Life at Brigham Young University, has argued that the key issue in life is not whether or how we either control or express our feelings. Rather, it has to do with the transfiguration of the feelings themselves. As he has observed:

> The quality of our emotions may be nothing more nor less than an expression of whether we are walking in the light. To walk in the light is the moral course. It is to honor the truths we know. To walk in darkness— including the emotions that attend contention—is to turn our backs on the light and knowledge we have received. The moral quality of our emotions changes when we live untruthfully. We then are hard-hearted. The scriptures say this more strongly: "Can ye be angry, and not sin?" (JST, Eph. 4:26). If some emotions are signals of wrongdoing, then when we give up our sin, our feelings should change in quality. At least the scriptures suggest this possibility: "Let all bitterness, and wrath, and anger, and clamour, and evil speaking, be put away from you, with all malice: and be ye kind one to another, tenderhearted, forgiving one another, even as God for Christ's sake hath forgiven you" (Ephesians 4:30–31).[93]

Under what conditions does this great change of heart typically take place in our lives? I believe it is as we confront the "necessary labors of the day" in the trenches of everyday living.

And how may we ensure that those daily labors are touched by grace and show forth grace? By making the Atonement operative in our life. At baptism, we were given the gift of the Holy Ghost—the great sanctifying power. The rule of the Holy Ghost is the kingdom of happiness, for He transforms the inner person so that we respond to external circumstances without letting those circumstances determine our inner being.

Is there a way, in the words of Alma, to daily "sing the song of redeeming love" and meet the necessary labors of the day with joy? What may we do? I return again to the advice of the prophets to those who have received the gift of the Holy Ghost. First, seek the perspective and revelations of heaven by a profound study of the scriptures. As Nephi said, "Angels speak by the power of the Holy Ghost; wherefore, they speak the words of Christ. Wherefore, I [say] unto you, feast upon the words of Christ; for behold, the words of Christ will tell you all things what ye should do" (2 Nephi 32:3).

President Spencer W. Kimball remarked, "I find that when I get casual in my relationship with divinity and when it seems that no divine ear is listening and no divine voice is speaking, that I am far, far away. If I immerse myself in the scriptures, the distance narrows and the spirituality returns. I find myself loving more intensely those whom I must love with all my heart and mind and strength, and loving them more. I find it easier to abide their counsel."[94] President Howard W. Hunter counseled that there be attentive, if brief, study of the scriptures each day rather than extended study only from time to time.[95]

After feasting upon the words of Christ, I would list as the second way in which we may meet with joy our daily tasks, living in accordance with what the Spirit testifies. If we wish to understand fully and taste the words of Christ, we must exert ourselves to conform all aspects of our lives to His. Giving sublime sermons will never make a man or woman holy; only a life in which we live what we teach will do so. Having received the light, let us walk in the light. And the light will grow until it fills and transforms our whole being.

In the midst of the great pentecostal spirit that prevailed in the days in which the Church was being organized, the Prophet Joseph Smith prayed at the dedication of the Kirtland Temple, "Remember all thy church, O Lord, with all their families, and all their immediate connections, with all their sick and afflicted ones, with all the poor and meek of the earth; that the kingdom, which thou hast set up without hands, may become a great mountain and fill the whole earth" (D&C 109:72). In all "our immediate connections," in the "necessary labors of the day," may that kingdom be reflected within us.

PART FOUR

TRUE FAITH

———•———

Exercising Faith in Christ

In withstanding evil and standing firm, nothing is more powerful than exercising faith in the Lord Jesus Christ. As we read in scripture, by such faith Abel offered an acceptable sacrifice to God, Enoch was translated that he did not see death, Noah prepared for a flood for which there was no evident harbinger, and Abraham left his home to journey to a land he did not know and later would have offered up his beloved Isaac as a sacrifice. By faith Isaac and Jacob blessed their posterities, Moses liberated Israel, the walls of Jericho fell, and the brother of Jared beheld the Lord.

Given all these examples and many more that could be cited, clearly faith is more than an opinion or even strong belief. It is not simply a logical conclusion derived from study and reasoning that there is a God or that Jesus is the Christ. Indeed, Paul defined faith as "the substance of things hoped for, the evidence of things not seen" or put another way, faith is the *assurance* of things hoped for and *proof* of things not seen (see Hebrews 11:1). Faith transcends the evidence of reason and the senses. It is centered in Jesus

Christ and entails not only an assurance that He is our Lord and Savior but also that we can rely on His promises.

Central to true faith is a willingness to show forth a witness of that profession and confidence in every aspect of our lives. This is the central message of James's great epistle. It was his invitation to those who lacked wisdom to ask of God, "nothing wavering," that inspired the boy Joseph Smith to pray, thus launching the inauguration of the dispensation of the fulness of times. James discerned faith in those who were doers of the word and not hearers only and who cared for the fatherless and the widow. He saw evidence of faith in those who bridled their tongues, sought peace, and ministered to the needs of others. James also detected the works of faith in the conversion of the unbeliever and sinner. He counseled those who would reduce faith to belief and a profession of the tongue:

> Thou believest that there is one God; thou doest well: the devils also believe, and tremble. But wilt thou know, O vain man, that faith without works is dead? Was not Abraham our father justified by works, when he had offered Isaac his son upon the altar? Seest thou how faith wrought with his works, and by works was faith made perfect? . . . For as the body without the spirit is dead, so faith without works is dead also. [James 2:19–22, 26]

Faith, then, is exemplified and perfected by showing forth Christ in all that we do.

But notice one other important aspect: the sacrifices we make, the time we consecrate, the talents and resources we contribute, the righteous choices we make—are all evidences of our faith in the promises of God and show a confidence that what we do is in accord with the mind and will of God. A "perfect brightness of hope" is also central to faith (see 2 Nephi 31:20). Faith banishes fear. Christ well expressed this in his admonition, "Be not afraid, only believe" (Mark 5:36). One of President Hinckley's favorite scriptures is Paul's declaration to Timothy, "For God hath not given us the spirit of fear; but of power, and of love, and of a sound mind" (2 Timothy 1:7).[96] It is interesting that Paul's affirmation of hope and confidence is in the same epistle in which he also prophesies that "in the last days perilous times shall come" (2 Timothy 3:1). Whatever the perils, putting our faith in Christ and acting according to His and the Father's will, we may decide and act with the same confidence that animated the ancient patriarchs.

Every day in large and small ways, each of us makes choices and undertakes "works" that reveal the source and depth of our faith. And, perhaps without thinking, we also act according to things not seen and with a confidence born of our reliance on Christ, His word, and the testimonies of His servants. Accepting a call to serve in a position for which one feels inadequate, resisting a temptation to cheat at school or in business, freely forgiving the unrepentant—these and many more decisions show forth not only honor but an abiding confidence in the Lord's promise, "and great shall be thy reward" (D&C 42:65).

During my second year, as an undergraduate at Stanford University, I received a call to serve a mission in France. I informed the dean of students that I would be withdrawing from the university at the end of the spring quarter. Shortly after leaving his office, I received a call from my advisor, a distinguished professor of philosophy, inviting me to his office. As soon as I walked though the door, he said, "Bob, are you crazy?" He then explained why it made no sense to interrupt my education and warned me there was no guarantee that I could get back into Stanford after being gone for two-and-a-half years (the length of a foreign language mission in those days). He concluded his argument by saying, "When you complete your studies, and if you still have this foolish notion, then you can do this mission thing!"

Now, aside from his obvious hostility to the very idea of serving a mission, my advisor made what seemed to be valid points. Why not complete my studies first? And it was true that there was no certainty that I could take up those studies again if I left for two-and-a-half-years. Yet, I knew I had been called by a prophet of God to be a full-time witness of Christ and His restored gospel in the French Mission. I could not predict or control what might happen after my mission, but I had the assurance of things hoped for, the evidence of things not seen.

Years later, I received another call from a prophet of God—this time to serve as a Seventy, to leave my career and with my wife go to a distant land. Shortly after accepting the call, I was sitting at my desk when a very senior official in the government burst into my office and asked, "Bob, are you crazy?" I told him that I had heard that same question many years before and, though his arguments had the same cogency as those earlier made by my academic advisor, I would once again put my confidence in the Lord and His servant.

I also remember that when I told the admiral for whom I was working that I would be leaving government service to accept a call from the Church, he jumped from his chair, grabbed the saber hanging on the wall above my head, and brandished it over me! He exclaimed, "You're going to do what?!" He was not entirely pleased with my decision! But he, a devout Catholic, later said to me, "I would have been disappointed in you had you made any other decision." In this, too, was an example of faith demonstrated and, if not completely understood, admired.

Every day in different ways we are each called by the Lord and His servants. It is our faith that dictates our response, and it is our response that magnifies our faith. To the world our responses must on occasion seem foolish. But even if we can't fully explain it to our incredulous nonmember friends, we can take comfort in what Paul meant when he observed, "God hath chosen the foolish things of the world to confound the wise" and that at last "the wisdom of the world is foolishness with God" (1 Corinthians 1:27; 3:19). Indeed, the establishment of the new and everlasting covenant in the latter days was to the end that "man should not counsel his fellowman, neither trust in the arm of flesh—But that every man might speak in the name of God the Lord, even the Savior of the world; that faith also might increase in the earth" (D&C 1:19–21).

In the two concluding chapters, we will consider the practical effect of true faith in our lives, as it is demonstrated in our willingness to stand as witnesses of Christ at all times and in all places and in a confidence that banishes fear. God will indeed be with us in the world, and we shall not fear but only believe.

CHAPTER 7

Without God in the World:
Avoiding Practical Atheism

Immediately after his conversion, Alma the Younger issued a warning to those who live "without God in the world" (Mosiah 27:31). At the beginning of this dispensation, the Lord also reflected on the pitiful condition of a world where "every man walketh in his own way, and after the image of his own god, whose image is in the likeness of the world, and whose substance is that of an idol" (D&C 1:16). Both on the level of the individual and of society, living without God in the world, or, if you will, effectively turning the substance of this world into our gods, has tragic consequences.

Reflecting on his own prior ignorance of God and His purposes, Alma speaks of having been in "the gall of bitterness and bonds of iniquity . . . in the darkest abyss" (Mosiah 27:29). And in declaring His reasons for restoring the gospel to the earth, the Lord in modern times explained it was to avoid the "calamity" of faithlessness that should otherwise have "come upon the inhabitants of the earth" (D&C 1:17). To preclude that calamity, the Lord revealed himself to Joseph Smith, gave commandments, restored to earth the priesthood and the organization of His church with the saving ordinances, and set His hand to once again establish his righteousness. In doing so, He authorized the "weak things of the world" who would not "trust in the arm of flesh" to speak "in the name of God the Lord, even the Savior of the world, *that faith also might increase in the earth* and that [His] everlasting covenant might be established" (D&C 1:19–22; emphasis added). This is the charge given to The Church of Jesus Christ of Latter-day Saints, and this is the call extended to every member of the Church. We must, each of us, in the privacy of our hearts and minds, ask whether our lives are grounded on the living God, or are there areas of our lives which are "without God in the world"?

"IF THE LORD BE GOD, FOLLOW HIM"

The word *atheist* comes from the Greek, *a theos,* which quite precisely means "without God." To be without God need not imply any explicit philosophical judgment or any profession of belief. Some may explicitly assume that it is desirable to conduct the life of society without any reference to a transcendent or eternal perspective. More generally, however, to be *a theos* may mean that we are in practice conducting the affairs of our personal and civic life without any consideration of the mind and will of God. Such ways of thinking and living may be called "practical atheism." Each of us should consider whether or not, despite our professions of faith, we might be living as practical atheists—and whether or not our nation trusts in God, as our national logo indicates, or whether we as a people are relying utterly upon the arm of flesh.

The scriptures and the living oracles of God proclaim that the Godhead whom we worship is at one and the same time **the God** of eternity, **the God of creation,** and **the God of history.** Men and women of faith submit themselves to a perfected and transcendent being—One constant in righteousness, understanding, concern, and care: "Glory, and honor, and power, and might, Be ascribed to our God; for he is full of mercy, Justice, grace and truth, and peace, forever and ever" (D&C 84:102). We who have embraced the restored gospel proclaim that God organized the world with purpose in mind and that all things that are owe their being to Him: "The worlds were made by him; men were made by him; all things were made by him, and through him, and of him" (D&C 93:10). We further testify that God acts within the affairs of men. The members of the godhead are personal beings and *God* is not a word for some cosmic law of consequences. The Son of God became flesh and dwelt among us, and God shall judge both men and nations: "And the Lord spake unto Moses, saying . . . Ye shall be holy: for I the Lord your God am holy" (Leviticus 19:1–2). This is the godhead under whose auspices we breathe and have life and who have commanded: "Thou shalt love the Lord thy God with all thy heart, with all thy might, mind, and strength; and in the name of Jesus Christ thou shalt serve him . . . And in nothing doth man offend God, or against none is his wrath kindled, save those who confess not his hand in all things, and obey not his commandments" (D&C 59:5, 21).

The superstitions of men, at times, portray divinity as a magical and arbitrary power whose ill-will is held at bay by confessions of the tongue and propitiations offered upon the altar. At other times, the philosophies of men transmute God into an abstract principle without body, parts, and passions—utterly immovable and remote from human concerns. But whether conceived of in superstition or philosophy, these false understandings ultimately destroy any sense of sin, guilt, judgment, or redemption—and those who embrace such beliefs find themselves without God in the world.

If we, however, hold that there is an absolute standard of righteousness that is apart from social mores and private desires, and if we further accept that this standard has been declared by a personal god, then all choices that we make in every realm of our lives must be driven by a desire to know God and His will. Jesus Christ declared the importance of our relationship to God when He taught: "This is life eternal, that they might know thee the only true God, and Jesus Christ, whom thou has sent" (John 17:3).

In *Lectures on Faith,* Joseph Smith expanded on this theme when he wrote:

> Let us here observe that three things are necessary in order that any rational and intelligent being may exercise faith in God unto life and salvation. First, the idea that He actually exists. Secondly, a correct idea of His character, perfections, and attributes. Thirdly, an actual knowledge that the course of life which he is pursuing is according to His will. For without acquaintance with these three important facts, the faith of every rational being must be imperfect and unproductive; but with this understanding it can become perfect and fruitful, abounding in righteousness, unto the praise of God the Father, and the Lord Jesus Christ.[97]

Thus, the greatest present happiness and our eternal destiny are both dependent on our discovering and following the will of God in the conduct of our society and most immediately in all the personal dimensions of our lives: our work, our recreations, our friendships, our loves, our families, and our stewardship as servants of Christ. What responsibilities does this imply?

AGENTS UNTO OURSELVES

The scriptures make clear that the purposes of mortality can only be realized if we are "agents unto ourselves." The root of the word *agency* means "to do" or "to act" and, in fact, moral agency is the freedom to do unconstrained by external compulsion, to act according to conscience and understanding. As the old hymn says:

> *For this eternal truth is giv'n:*
> *That God will force no man to heav'n,*
> *He'll call, persuade, direct aright,*
> *And bless with wisdom, love, and light,*
> *In nameless ways be good and kind,*
> *But never force the human mind.*[98]

Joseph Smith utilized this principle in leading the Latter-day Saints. When asked about his technique, he replied, "I teach them correct principles, and they govern themselves."[99]

Have you often wondered why God counsels us to seek Him, to knock at the door? The plan of salvation dictates that much of the initiative lies with us. He asks us to study out a problem in our mind, guided by divine principles and shaped by prayer. God will not shout orders nor compel behavior. He will declare divine commandments to guide our actions and will in the resolution of specific issues point the way through the whisperings of the Spirit—but He will never do it in a way that would violate our agency.

It is worth noting that God has always established His relationship with His people and with each of us as individuals through covenants. A covenant is premised on free choice and recognizes the responsible character of the parties. The commandments given to Israel were preceded by the covenant with

Abraham, Isaac, and Jacob and with the agreement made under Moses' leadership that they, the people of Israel, would accept *the* God as their god and would be His people. The law of the gospel of Jesus Christ was based upon the new and everlasting covenant. We accept on a personal basis the commands of God and the guidance of the Holy Ghost by the covenant we make in baptism. God will only lead in freedom.

Reaching our fullest potential and achieving that effectiveness can be done only by aligning our will freely with that of our Father in Heaven. And how do we discover His will? We must ponder the scriptures, listen to the living prophets, and humble ourselves in prayer before God. Whatever the issue, we need to consult the scriptures, which contain the rules of moral conduct decreed by heaven, emulate Christ's example, and prayerfully seek to know God's will—and then we must align our lives with this understanding.

Moral reasoning is not easy, for it involves not only defining principles, rules, and purposes but also applying our discoveries in the real events of our lives. If we are to be perfected in righteousness, God will seldom force an answer upon us but will, as a wise teacher, guide our reason and confirm our labors. There are no cookbooks for every situation, no magic formulas, but there are "do's" and "don'ts," parables and cautionary tales, divinely-decreed goals, and inspired guidelines. To know God and Jesus Christ whom He has sent requires constant effort. To ascertain His will requires all of our heart, might, mind, and strength. This effort and this submission is the only way by which we will be with God in the world—until at last we can say, with Paul, that we have the "mind of Christ" (1 Corinthians 2:16).

Ammon counseled that we pray "continually without ceasing" (Alma 26:22).

Amulek urged that we cry unto the Lord in all the decisions and acts of our lives, that our hearts be fully "drawn out in prayer unto him continually for [our] welfare, and also for the welfare of those who are around [us]" (Alma 34:27). No advice could be more powerful for any who are tempted to act without counseling with God than the words of Alma to Helaman:

> O, remember, my son, and learn wisdom in thy youth; yea, learn in thy youth to keep the commandments of God. Yea, and cry unto God for all thy support; yea, let all thy doings be unto the Lord, and whithersoever thou goest let it be in the Lord; yea, let all thy thoughts be directed unto the Lord; yea, let the affections of thy heart be placed upon the Lord forever. Counsel with the Lord in all thy doings, and he will direct thee for good; yea, when thou liest down at night lie down unto the Lord, that he may watch over you in your sleep; and when thou risest in the morning let thy heart be full of thanks unto God; and if ye do these things, ye shall be lifted up at the last day. [Alma 37:35–37]

GOD IN OUR WORLD: ETERNITY IN TIME

If God is to be with us in the world, our hearts must be continually drawn out in prayer toward ascertaining the mind and will of God. To fully grasp the things of time we must have the perspective of eternity. I can think of no aspect of our life that should not be scrutinized from this perspective: our relationships; our jobs and professions; our lives as students; our roles as husband, wife, mother, father, child, sibling; our hobbies and recreation; our civic duties; our Church responsibilities. In every aspect of life, the standard is clear: "Therefore," asked the resurrected Christ, "what manner of men ought ye to be? Verily I say unto you, even as I am" (3 Nephi 27:27).

Relationships

First, let us consider relationships. There is no theme so central to the Christian message than that we must love our neighbor. We *are* our brother's keepers. I take this to mean that in one way or another we are either assisting or impeding each other on the road toward eternal perfection. I tremble to think that my words and my actions may so wound the spirit of another as to darken his or her vision of celestial glory. Whether at work, at play, in the streets and byways of daily commerce, or in the sanctuary of God, our work and our glory, as it is with God, must be to bring to pass the eternal life of our fellowman.

Family Life

If this be "our work and glory" among our fellow men, how much more is it so with our spouses and families? Marriage and family life is a relationship established by a sacred covenant—an agreement in holiness. The family is the central matrix of the gospel, the context within which the principles of sacrifice and of consecration are developed and exemplified most intensely. It is the primary stage upon which we act out the Christ-like life.

There are no guarantees that our devotion will transform for good every member of the family. Christ himself cannot exalt every man and woman; for, in every sphere of mortal existence, including the family, we remain agents unto ourselves. This fact, at once melancholy and glorious, does not remove from any one of us the charge of acting within the family as Christ does toward all mankind. I think it is for this reason that the Apostle Paul used the analogy of marriage in describing the relationship of Christ to his people and used the life of Christ in describing marriage: "Husbands, love your wives, even as Christ also loved the church, and gave himself for it . . . and the wife see that she reverence her husband. Children, obey your parents in the Lord: for this is right. Honour thy father and mother . . . And, ye fathers, provoke not your children to wrath: but bring them up in the nurture and admonition of the Lord" (Ephesians 5:25, 33; 6:1–2, 4). I find it significant that it is in the context of family life that Paul utters that familiar and moving call: "My brethren, be strong in the Lord, and in the power of his might. Put on the whole armour of God, that ye may be able to stand against the wiles of the devil . . . that ye may be able to withstand the evil day, and having done all, to stand" (Ephesians 6:10–11, 13). If anyone counsels any differing approach to husband, to wife, to parents, and to children, they have not the "mind of Christ."

The Workplace

In the business of making a living, we must also take great care that we do not find ourselves without God in the world. Much of our lives will be spent earning our bread. Therefore, the nature of our relationships and many aspects of our personality will be evident in the marketplace.

The issue is not what we *do* to make a living so much as whether the work is honorable—not only within the bounds of secular law but shaped by the inspiration of Sinai and of Gethsemane. The excuse that "everyone is doing it" is no more acceptable from an adult in business than from a teenager in school. Not only must our work be honorable, but we must be honest in the performance of our duties and tasks: we must be diligent in performing our assignments; we must apply the principles of the Sermon on the Mount to employer, employee, and customer alike. Neither greed nor desperation should govern our actions.

I suspect that all of us need to reflect on our behavior in this area, and where repentance is required, we should not procrastinate. Some may say that the standards of heaven cannot be applied to the competitive world of business. It is true that every man and woman must seek diligently the inspiration of God in how these standards are applied in particular circumstances, but there can be no doubt that the rules of redemption are not suspended during business hours.

The Schoolhouse

You who are called to be students, young and old, you also must pursue your education under the inspiration and guidance of heaven. At the main entrance to Brigham Young University, there are inscribed these words of revelation: "The glory of God is intelligence, or, in other words, light and truth" (D&C 93:36). As many of you have discovered, the excitement of true learning is not simply gathering diverse bits of information but learning to understand how they fit into a pattern and how that pattern reveals the hand of God. Such patterns elucidate, and such light represents the truth that shall make us free. That may be in part what the Lord was teaching us when He inspired the Prophet Joseph Smith to observe, "It is impossible for a man to be saved in ignorance" (D&C 131:6).

The knowledge that saves ultimately encompasses the whole universe. As God has counseled in Latter-day revelation: "And, verily I say unto you, that it is my will that you should . . . obtain a knowledge of history, and of countries, and of kingdoms, of laws of God and man, . . . of things both in heaven and in the earth, and under the earth; things which have been, things which are, things which must shortly come to pass; things which are at home, things which are abroad. . . . That ye may be prepared in all things . . . to magnify the calling whereunto I have called you" (D&C 93:53; 88:79–80).

Students, bring all your energy, all your intellect, all your diligence to your studies. If you do so, seeking the aid of the Holy Ghost and obeying the commandments of your Heavenly Father, your minds will be bathed in light, and you shall begin to see as the Lord sees.

Recreation

Much of life is taken up with what we call *pleasure* or *leisure*. Who has not been ennobled by music, dance, drama, arts, sculpture, painting, soaring architecture, or powerful language? But these artistic expressions can also debase as well as ennoble.

True understanding and righteous living, what the ancient Greeks called the *true* and the *good*, are often revealed and strengthened by artistic expression—the *beautiful*. All men are born with the Light of Christ, and it is that intuition of the soul that has led the poets, the artists, the musicians of the ages to pierce the defects of their own understanding and desires and to illuminate in exalted expression the profound harmony of the universe. This intuition of the soul, this Light of Christ, made visible in great art, opens to mankind the eye of understanding and inspires the way of righteousness. Here, too, in re-creation, creating ourselves anew, we may be with God in the world. This being the case, we must also understand that Satan, the father of lies, seeks not only to darken our understanding and to entice us to do evil, but also to debase the intuition of our souls, pervert our aesthetic sensibilities, and prostitute our emotions in order to diminish the Light of Christ.

Satan seeks not only to persuade that false is true and evil is good but also to so corrupt our intuitions that we perceive ugly as beautiful. In many respects, it is this debasement of our emotions, our intuition, and our artistic sense that is most dangerous, for, while we are embracing these counterfeit emotions we may cloak the Light of Christ within. Ignorance may be cured by enlightenment, sin may be overcome by repentance, but, if the feelings and the sense of proportion and reverence that undergird true beauty are corrupted, the very ability to recognize truth and the desire to do good may be utterly suppressed. In the matter of our recreation and entertainments, therefore, let us harken to the words of Moroni:

> Wherefore, all things which are good cometh of God; and that which is evil cometh of the devil; for the devil is an enemy unto God, and fighteth against him continually, and inviteth and enticeth to sin, and to do that which is evil continually. But behold, that which is of God inviteth and enticeth to do good continually; wherefore, every thing which inviteth and enticeth to do good, and to love God, and to serve him, is inspired of God. [Moroni 7:12–13]

THE CIVIC CULTURE

If our happiness and success as individuals depend utterly on our searching out and following the will of God, so too does the welfare of our community depend on being with God in the world. The founders of this democratic republic knew that the redemption not only of each individual but of the nation collectively depended on submission to God.

One of the inspirations for the great ideas undergirding the American Declaration of Independence and U.S. Constitution was the thinking of John Locke, the British political and social philosopher (1632–1704). In his famous *A Letter Concerning Toleration* (1689), he asked: "Can a person who does not acknowledge that he is accountable to a truth higher than the self, external to the self, really be trusted?" And he replied to his query: "Promises, covenants, and oaths, which are the bonds of human society, can have no hold upon an atheist. The taking away of God, though but even in thought, dissolves all."[100] James Madison, the principal author of the Constitution, accepted this proposition and, along with the other founders of the republic, believed that religious freedom is an inalienable right based upon an inalienable duty. As he wrote in 1785:

> It is the duty of every man to render to the Creator such homage and such only as he believe to be acceptable to [God]. This duty is precedent, both in order of time and in degree of obligation, to the claims of Civil Society. Before any man can be considered as a member of Civil Society, he must be considered as a subject of the Governour of the Universe: And if a member of Civil Society, who enters into any subordinate Association, must always do it with a reservation of his duty to General Authority; much more must every man who becomes a member of any particular Civil Society, do it with a saving of his allegiance to the Universal Sovereign.[101]

One may think that Locke's explicit and Madison's implicit mistrust of atheists is a bit harsh, for surely there are good and

honest atheists in whom trust may be reposed. The central philosophical point has, however, great power. If there is no objective
order of truth and right outside of any particular individual or
society against which we can measure our beliefs and acts, then
truth and right are but ephemeral agreements, imposed either by
consensus or by coercion. Those who accept this belief must necessarily feel less transcendent constraint upon their behavior. Like
Korihor in the Book of Mormon, they tend to conclude that
"every man fare[s] in this life according to the management of the
creature; therefore every man prosper[s] according to his genius,
and that every man conquer[s] according to his strength; and
whatsoever a man [does is] no crime" (Alma 30:17).

The Founders believed that the social contract that we called
The Constitution of the United States was not simply a con-
trivance of convergent or balanced self-interests but a covenant
aimed at the realization of a society of free men and women striving toward a dignified life and moral perfection. So overwhelmed
were they with the sense that the principles of this republic would
transform history, that they referred to the product of their constitutional effort as a *novus ordo seclorum*—a new order of the
ages.[102] The Constitution, in Abraham Lincoln's magisterial words,
was not simply a "deal struck" but a covenant of a nation "so
conceived and so dedicated." [103]

Alexis de Tocqueville, the early nineteenth-century French
author of *Democracy in America,* the greatest study ever done on
American society, perceived the link that Madison forged and
Lincoln celebrated between a free civil society and subjection to
God. He wrote:

> American civilization is the result . . . of two distinct
> elements, which in other places have been in frequent dis-
> agreement, but which the Americans have succeeded in

incorporating to some extent one with the other and combining admirably. I allude to the spirit of religion and the spirit of liberty. . . . Religion perceives that civil liberty affords a noble exercise to the faculties of man and that the political world is a field prepared by the Creator for the efforts of mind. Free and powerful in its own sphere, satisfied with the place reserved for it, religion never more surely establishes its empire than when it reigns in the hearts of men unsupported by aught beside its native strength. Liberty regards religion as its companion in all its battles and its triumphs, as the cradle of its infancy and the divine source of its claims. It considers religion as the safeguard of morality, and morality as the best security of law and the surest pledge of the duration of freedom. . . . Despotism may govern without faith, but liberty cannot . . . How is it possible that society should escape destruction if the moral tie is not strengthened in proportion as the political tie is relaxed? And what can be done with a people who are their own masters if they are not submissive to the Deity?[104]

Believers in the God of Abraham, Isaac, and Jacob and followers of Jesus Christ the Son of the Living God are and should be the best citizens precisely because they understand that loyalty to civil society is qualified by a higher loyalty to the God who transcends history and stands as judge of this republic and its people.

Latter-day Saints are aware of the proclamation of The Book of Mormon that Jesus Christ is the God of this land. Our freedom has been vouchsafed by God, if the inhabitants of this blessed land "serve him according to the commandments which he hath given" (2 Nephi 1:7). The manner in which we exercise that freedom will be subject to the judgment of heaven. Thomas Jefferson expressed that sense of judgment when he remarked that "I tremble for the fate of my nation when I realize that God is just."[105]

This republic was founded on the premise that the state may make only a sharply limited claim upon the loyalty of its citizens. Not only must the state eschew any attempt to prescribe or favor any particular religious creed, but it must also take care not to exercise power or to expend public funds in the promotion of ideas and practices that deny the hand of God in all things. The practice of creedal neutrality is at the heart of the United States Constitution, but so also is trust in a divine judge who stands above the republic.

Latter-day Saints understand this and will expend time, treasure, and life itself to defend this republic "so conceived and so dedicated." In revelation, Lehi saw the hand of God in the founding of this republic in order that a free civil order might be established. The resulting political order would provide the social context within which the Lord would begin a marvelous work and a wonder—the restoration of the Church and kingdom of God and the establishment of a base for the preaching of the gospel for the last time to the entire world.

Speaking of that constitution, the God of heaven proclaimed in this day that He had "suffered [it] to be established" and that it was to be maintained "for the rights and protection of all flesh, according to just and holy principles" (D&C 101:77). It is the duty, therefore, of all Americans to preserve this divinely inspired covenant, and it is particularly incumbent upon the Latter-day Saints to participate as engaged citizens in the defense of the liberties so established and in defense of the just and holy principles that both sustain and justify those liberties.

As citizens of the American republic and as fellow-citizens of the household of faith, we must hold our public servants account-able not only for their political and administrative competence but also for their willingness to acknowledge and follow a standard of righteousness, which they did not invent but by which we all will be judged.

VISIONS OF GLORY

In our national life and our personal lives, then, we must seek the hand of God in all things and freely bend our will to His. In his famous charge to his son Corianton, Alma described this life as "a time to repent and serve God" (Alma 42:4). How simple this is and how oft ignored, yet the consequences of failing to adhere to this uncomplicated counsel are immense.

Remember again what the Apostle Paul wrote in his epistle to the Romans: "And be not conformed to this world: but be ye transformed by the renewing of your mind, that ye may prove what is that good, and acceptable, and perfect, will of God" (Romans 12:2). The world that excludes God holds promises unfulfilled and joys incomplete. But if, in all the challenges and struggles of life, we seek the living God, all bitterness will at last become sweet and all disappointments swept away in a vision of glory. As the Lord declared: "Wherefore, fear not even unto death; for in this world your joy is not full, but in me your joy is full. . . . Seek the face of the Lord always, that in patience ye may possess your souls, and ye shall have eternal life" (D&C 101:35, 38).

CHAPTER 8

Avoiding Heart Failure
in Troubled Times

Within our family walls and in the walks of our daily life, we are constantly reminded that, even in the sunlight of peace, the shadow of strife and war looms. How do we understand the troubled times in which we live, and what counsel do we take one with another and with those over whom we have stewardship?

In late December 1832 and early January 1833, the Prophet Joseph Smith received an extensive and marvelous revelation, which he designated as the "olive leaf . . . plucked from the Tree of Paradise, the Lord's message of peace to us" (see preface to D&C 88). In this revelation, the Lord pronounces the Saints to be his "friends" and declares that the Holy Ghost, which is the Comforter, will implant in the hearts of the Saints the promise of eternal life, "even the glory of the celestial kingdom; Which glory is that of the church of the Firstborn, even of God, the holiest of all, through Jesus Christ his son" (D&C 88:3–5). In this revelation, the Lord speaks of the laws and conditions of this kingdom, summons us to sanctify ourselves so that our minds will be single to the glory of God, and promises that "he that seeketh me early shall find me, and shall not be forsaken" (see v. 83).

The Lord commands us to gain knowledge of all things, even "the wars and the perplexities of nations" (v.79) and directs us to testify and warn the nations (v. 81), to entangle not ourselves in sin (see v. 86), and to prepare for the "voice of thunderings, and the voice of lightnings, and the voice of tempests, and the voice of the waves of the sea heaving themselves beyond their bounds. And all things shall be in commotion; and surely, men's hearts shall fail them; for fear shall come upon all people" (vv. 90–91).

Wherein, then, lies "the Lord's message of peace" in this litany of ills and blanket of darkness? The Lord answers:

> And if your eye be single to my glory, your whole bodies shall be filled with light, and there shall be no darkness in you; and that body which is filled with light comprehendeth all things. Therefore, sanctify yourselves that your minds become single to God, and the days will come that you shall see him; for he will unveil his face unto you, and it shall be in his own time, and in his own way, and according to his own will. Remember the great and last promise which I have made unto you. [D&C 88:67–69]

And so the Lord points to the tumultuous circumstance of our age *and* to the promise of peace within. As the angel proclaimed Christ's birth to shepherds who "were sore afraid" with the words "fear not" (Luke 2:9–10), and as Christ concluded his mortal ministry with the words, "Peace I leave with you, my peace I give unto you: not as the world giveth, give I unto you. Let not your heart be troubled, neither let it be afraid" (John 14:27), so, at the beginning of the final dispensation, the Lord spoke of peace in the midst of war:

The enemy in the secret chambers seeketh your lives. Ye hear of wars in far countries, and you say that there will soon be great wars in far countries, but ye know not the hearts of men in your own land . . . treasure up wisdom in your bosoms, lest the wickedness of men reveal these things unto you by their wickedness, in a manner which shall speak in your ears with a voice louder than that which shall shake the earth; but if ye are prepared ye shall not fear. . . . Behold, verily, verily, I say unto you that mine eyes are upon you. I am in your midst and ye cannot see me; But the day soon cometh that ye shall see me, and know that I am; for the veil of darkness shall soon be rent, and he that is not purified shall not abide the day. Wherefore, gird up your loins and be prepared. Behold, the kingdom is yours, and the enemy shall not overcome. [D&C 38:28–30; 7–9]

The mundane challenges of daily life and the cataclysmic disasters of nature and of men threaten to overwhelm. Indeed, at the 1958 dedication of the London Temple, President David O. McKay spoke of a growing anxiety that would grip all mankind, a force emanating from the mind of Satan, causing men to fear. Fear, anxiety, a troubled heart—for many, these seem near at hand; for some, these emotions are a constant brooding presence. But, as the Lord declared, crushing fear arises not from the perils of circumstance but from the failure of a heart separated from God.

In another troubled time, Moses spoke of the fear experienced by a nation no longer grounded on the rock of salvation, the Holy One of Israel:

The sword without, and terror within, shall destroy both the young man and the virgin, the suckling also with the man of gray hairs . . . For they are a nation void of counsel, neither is there any understanding in them. O that they were wise, that they understood this, that they would consider their latter end! [Deuteronomy 32:25, 28–29]

It is the character of our soul, not the circumstances of our life, that holds the key to the banishment of fear and the establishment of the kingdom of peace within. As Christ counseled his ancient apostles: "And fear not them which kill the body, but are not able to kill the soul: but rather fear him which is able to destroy both soul and body in hell" (Matthew 10:28).

The latter-day prophets, speaking with "the perfect love that casteth out fear" (1 John 4:18), have consistently and persistently declared the way of peace in the midst of distress, present and future, expected and unexpected. Let us consider some of this inspired counsel. I would here group together in two categories this prophetic counsel:

First, be prepared and, second, build upon an unshakeable foundation. Whether it be in our family or in our wards and stakes or in our communities, these two things are critical: be prepared and establish a firm foundation.

Be Prepared

Wait not upon events, but reflect, work, and prepare to deal with them. There are at least three ways to think about the future: in terms of trends, contingencies, and our purposes. If we think from the point of view of trends, we tend to project the forces and activities that we currently observe. In effect, we see the future as an extension of the present. The problem, of course, is to accurately determine those forces or activities that will endure and be decisive in the future.

Another way of thinking about the future is to consider contingencies—possible but uncertain or unlikely happenings: floods, wars, economic downturns or, on the positive side, opportunities for better work, more education, and an inheritance. The challenge here is to prepare ourselves to minimize the worst and accentuate the best, should these events actually transpire.

Finally, we think of the future in terms of our purposes. In other words, we seek to define the principles and objectives that will help us mold the future and control our choices. The problem in this case is to identify those principles that endure through changing circumstances and to establish priority among our goals.

Whether because of trends, contingencies, or purposes, our real aim is to develop a sense of confidence before uncertainty. To attain such confidence, we must first understand that we cannot predict the future, but may prepare for it by developing our personal and family attributes and taking prudential steps to minimize dangers to our well-being and maximize our flexibility in different circumstances.

The outcome of the difficulties or opportunities that we may face depend less on the nature of those situations or events than on our capacity to respond positively and effectively.

I have a friend whose father was a very successful attorney in the Midwest. Doctors discovered that my friend's father had a form of cancer—one that spreads slowly and would likely have minimal effect for fifteen or twenty years. At the age of 80, this man would probably die before the cancer could kill him! But he was so shocked and depressed by the very idea of having cancer that he, in fact, died two weeks after the initial diagnosis.

On the other hand, this same friend has a daughter who, at age three, was diagnosed with a particularly virulent and horrible cancer that almost always proves to be fatal. But the doctors said that they had never seen a child with such a strong physical constitution and emotional strength. In fact, this child conquered the disease and as of this writing is fourteen years old.

In these two cases, the trauma was not the problem but the pre-existent physical and emotional conditions of each person. The personal state was more important than the external challenge. Likewise, in other spheres, our personal or family condition may be the decisive factor in determining the outcome of a difficulty or opportunity.

Our acquired attributes and skills, as well as our personal and family strengths and weaknesses, may be of decisive importance in our ability to cope with challenges and to seize opportunities. The best security for the future and our present peace of mind may be found in who we are, what we can do, and the prudential steps we have taken to minimize risk and expand our margin of error, along with the strength of our principles and the adequacy of our goals.

The prophets have summoned us to build our individual and family strengths so that whether the future holds raging storms or sunlit paths, we are prepared and need not fear. And what are some of the things they have asked us to do? They are so simple that many may have looked well beyond the mark. We know them well, but are we following this counsel?

1. Strengthen the family as the central institution of our society. Secure it from the assaults of selfishness within and the crude and lewd noises from without. I would commend "The Family: A Proclamation to the World"[106] as the foundation of our personal counsel and family councils. It is the product of the inspired insights of prophets, seers, and revelators, who see the very foundations of civilized life beginning to crumble.

2. Identify and develop divine attributes. The Apostle Peter summoned those who have come to "the knowledge of God and of Jesus our Lord" and have been given all things that "pertain unto life and godliness," to realize the potential of their divine nature by giving all diligence to the development of faith, virtue, knowledge, temperance, patience, godliness, brotherly kindness, and charity. Should they do this, their knowledge of Christ will be full and fruitful, they shall see "afar off," and they "shall never fall" (2 Peter 1:2–10). Again, who we are is more decisive than what may happen.

3. Keep our eye on the ball. Be guided by eternal purposes and do not be so diverted by the journey of life, including the storms and the gales, that we forget why we came into mortality and to what we should be tending.

4. Establish priorities. The key to a successful life is not simply choosing between things that are good and bad in themselves but deciding, as among good things, what is more important. The sure guide is to seek first the kingdom of God and its righteousness (Matthew 6:33) and to be guided also by the principles of sacrifice and consecration. And we must be ever attentive to the injunction that "if we do not improve our time while in this life, then cometh the night of darkness wherein there can be no labor performed" (Alma 34:33).

5. Strengthen the temporal foundations of our life. Our material circumstances cannot in themselves shield us from uncertainty or disaster, nor can they insure our happiness. On the other hand, inattention to the material sinews of our life will expose us to any shift in the winds of fortune and limit our ability to pursue noble goals.

This is why with ever greater urgency the prophets have counseled us to protect and strengthen the physical body the Lord has granted us. The Word of Wisdom provides a standard by which we can evaluate issues pertaining to the health of the body. The ability even to think and to deal with the normal stresses of life is critically influenced by the care we take of our mortal beings. Indeed, not only may we walk and not be weary, but the Lord has promised us that treasures of hidden truth will be revealed to us as we properly care for and reverence the body, which has been designated a temple where the Holy Spirit may abide (see D&C 89; 1 Corinthians 3:16).

We are also urgently advised to improve our powers of thought and communication and to develop specialized skills and to cultivate work habits that will enable us to deal successfully with a changing marketplace.

The prophets have also counseled us to get out of debt. This means reducing consumption and building a margin of security into our financial affairs, however modest. We have been urged as well to build up necessary reserves to take care of the necessities of life in the event of unforeseen circumstances, failing health, or loss of employment. Storage of food and other items is simply a prudential step to guard against the perils of uncertainty and social disruptions.

Finally, there are principles of temporal salvation with immediate eternal consequences, such as the payment of an honest tithe and observing a true fast that will allow us to help alleviate the want and suffering of others. It is a remarkable fact that our willingness to bear one another's burdens and to join together in great enterprises to advance the kingdom of God upon the earth strengthens not only the whole of the Church but also each of us individually. Although we must develop traits of self-reliance, which is really taking personal responsibility, we are never entirely self-sufficient. We rely on the mercies of our Heavenly Father but have also been counseled to buoy each other up and to be "anxiously engaged in a good cause" beyond our personal concerns, helping to "bring to pass much righteousness" (D&C 58:27).

Physical fitness, education, prudent financial management, provident living, storage of essential provisions, and the honest payment of tithes and offerings—these are critical conditions by which we not only secure our present situation but also protect ourselves against the inevitable fluctuations in circumstances. As a prudent nation prepares for war in time of peace, so a wise individual prepares for personal and family challenges in time of prosperity.

6. **Do not judge and do forgive.** The burden of sitting in judgment of people and circumstances is the province of those who have been designated by the Lord to be "judges in Israel." Those not so called are counseled by the Lord: "Judge not, that ye be not judged." (Matthew 7:1). Indeed, the Lord expanded that declaration by reminding us that rather than criticize another, we ought to concentrate instead on ridding ourselves of our own deficiencies: "First cast out the beam out of thine own eye; and then shalt thou see clearly to cast out the mote out of thy brother's eye" (Matthew 7:5). Moreover, when we forgive or refrain from criticizing or bearing grudges for hurts, real or imagined, we decrease the stress and annoyances that rob us of the peace we might otherwise enjoy.

7. **Be positive.** During his imprisonment in Liberty Jail, a time of great suffering and duress, Joseph Smith gave this wonderful counsel to the Saints: "Therefore, dearly beloved brethren, let us cheerfully do all things that lie in our power; and then may

we stand still, with the utmost assurance, to see the salvation of God, and for his arm to be revealed" (D&C 123:17).

Build upon an Unshakeable Foundation

The second category of prophetic counsel pertains to the foundation on which we rest our faith. Helaman stated the matter most clearly: "Remember, remember that it is upon the rock of our Redeemer, who is Christ, the Son of God, that ye must build your foundation" (Helaman 5:12).

The French philosopher and mathematician Blaise Pascal (1623–62) wrote:

> There is a virtuous fear which is the effect of faith and a vicious fear which is the product of doubt and distrust. The former leads to hope as relying on God in whom we believe; the latter inclines to despair, as not relying upon God, in whom we do not believe. Persons of one character fear to lose God; those of the other character fear to find him.[107]

What are the conditions of such faith and "virtuous fear"? In *Lectures on Faith,* prepared under the direction of the Prophet Joseph Smith, we read:

> From the first existence of man, the faith necessary unto the enjoyment of life and salvation never could be obtained without the sacrifice of all earthly things. . . . But those who have not made this sacrifice to God do not know that the course which they pursue is well pleasing in his sight; for whatever may be their belief or their opinion, it is a matter of doubt and uncertainty in their mind; and where doubt and uncertainty are, there faith is not,

nor can it be. For doubt and faith do not exist in the same person at the same time; so that persons whose minds are under doubt and fears cannot have unshaken confidence; and where unshaken confidence is not, there faith is weak; and where faith is weak, the persons will not be able to contend against all the oppositions, tribulations, and afflictions which they will have to encounter in order to be heirs of God, and joint heirs with Christ Jesus; and they will grow weary in their minds, and the adversary will have power over them and destroy them.[108]

It is this understanding of the nature of life and this view of faith that is reflected in Christ's counsel to his apostles: "And fear not them which kill the body, but are not able to kill the soul: but rather fear him which is able to destroy both soul and body in hell" (Matthew 10:28). Faith in Christ—knowing not only that He *is* but relying upon Him—is the foundation of peace and the bulwark against fear and despair.

He who was about to undergo the agony of Gethsemane and Golgotha blessed His apostles: "Peace I leave with you, my peace I give unto you: not as the world giveth, give I unto you. Let not your heart be troubled, neither let it be afraid" (John 14:27). Built upon the foundation, which is Christ, and obedient to the counsel of His holy prophets and apostles, we may know this peace, and we may affirm with Paul, "God hath not given us the spirit of fear; but of power, and of love, and of a sound mind" (2 Timothy 1:7).

CONCLUSION

Better Than You Are

In the 1944 hit movie *Going My Way*, Bing Crosby sings a tune called "Swinging on a Star." The lyrics of the song call upon us to be better than we are and compares such an aspiration to settling for something far less than we as human beings are capable of becoming: "Would you like to swing on a star, carry moonbeams home in a jar, and be better off than you are, or would you rather be a mule?" Crosby compares those who aspire to less than they can achieve to a number of other animals. He then concludes by singing, "So you see, it's all up to you. You could be better than you are. You could be swinging on a star."[109]

Over the previous chapters we have considered how we as Latter-day Saints represent in our lives the truth that has sprung forth from the earth and the righteousness sent down from heaven. To help us withstand the destructive forces of the latter days, we have been counseled to put on the whole armor of God. And we have considered together four dimensions of that armor—true understanding, true character, true discipleship, and true faith. So protected, we are called forth as instruments to help further a great work that is to sweep the earth as a mighty flood. We are summoned to realize the possibilities that are in each one of us.

We all want to be better than we are. If you doubt that, pay attention to the self-improvement section in any bookstore. There are so many books that presume to explain how we can improve our behavior or outlook, on every conceivable level, and the number of such books keeps growing. This demonstrates two things: first, that we *do* want to be better than we are and, second, that we're having difficulty doing so.

What, then, is to be done? I believe mortal happiness, as well as eternal fulfillment, lies in the *quest* to fulfill that which is best within us, to become better than we are. But the constant addition of new books to the self-improvement shelves indicates that our quest to overcome problems and foibles and to develop our strengths and joys is not yet satisfied—and, I suggest, will never be satisfied until we turn both inward toward our potential and outward toward service to God and fellowman.

First, we need to look toward what the classical philosophers have called the "virtues," that is, the admirable traits, characteristics, and possibilities that lie within us as sons and daughters of our Heavenly Father and which we must cultivate if we are to meet the full measure of our creation and know lasting joy. We have the potential to grow into the image of Him who made us in His image.

Note one important fact: the possibility that we have of becoming perfected also implies that we have the possibility of being a good deal worse than we are. The power of perfectibility is also the power of corruptibility. When someone says your possibilities are limitless, they are near the mark, but let us understand that those possibilities move in both directions. We can be so sanctified that we show forth in our countenance the image of the divine, but we may also be so corrupted that we show forth in our countenance the image of him who is the father of lies.

Our Heavenly Father intends for us to progress in righteousness toward becoming as He is—to be perfected. Some scoff at that elevated view of man, but that is the counsel that Christ gave in the Sermon on the Mount: "Be ye therefore perfect, even as your Father which is in heaven is perfect" (Matthew 5:48). Is it unreasonable to believe that as spiritual offspring of divine parents, we may grow into their image, which is imprinted upon us, and become coheirs with Christ of the glory of the Father? Because of the effects of the Fall and our own corruptibility as mortal men and women, without the intervention of Christ and the marvelous blessings of the Atonement and the Resurrection, we could never by our own devices reach that state.

But we must also do all that we are capable of doing to develop the divine traits or virtues within us and bring them into full flower.

Many years ago typesetters for printing presses, who had to place the letters *p* and *q* backwards on the printing block so that they would come out properly on the printed page, were cautioned "to mind their p's and q's"—so they would not reverse them. Minding one's p's and q's has since become an expression reminding us to get it right. In conclusion, I would draw attention to five p's and two q's that we need to get right if we are to become better than we are. They are:

Picture
Practice
Priorities
Prayer
Persistence

Quest
Quietude

Picture

We need to visualize and focus on those traits we wish to develop, but we need to move beyond abstractions. We must personalize those traits, to have a picture in our minds, in order to actualize and to be able to apply in our lives virtuous characteristics. Images, models, pictures, and visible heroes, if you will, are very important. In my office at work and in my study at home are a number of pictures that keep me focused on individuals I would like to emulate: Thomas Jefferson, James Madison, Abraham Lincoln, the Prophet Joseph Smith, members of The First Presidency and the Quorum of the Twelve, and members of my family. Each of these individuals possesses some or many noble traits that I would like to incorporate into my life. Their photographs or depictions make concrete that which is "virtuous, lovely, or of good report or praiseworthy." In one way or another, when I focus on those images, I see in human terms the possibility of being "honest, true, chaste, benevolent, virtuous, and . . . doing good to all men" (Articles of Faith 1:13).

You may recall Nathaniel Hawthorne's famous story entitled "The Great Stone Face," in which the author describes the image of a man's face that had been carved by nature into one of the cliffs of the White Mountains in New Hampshire. Many who viewed the image saw mirrored in it the nobility of a great soul, one filled with virtuous and kindly traits. Legend had it that there would one day come to the village an actual person who would possess all those attributes and be the living reflection of the great stone face.

There was a boy named Ernest, who grew up in the shadow

of that visage. He was attracted to it and drawn to develop the virtuous traits that he saw reflected there. Ernest grew up, left home, and made his way in the world. At last he retired back to the valleys and hills of New Hampshire. When he returned, the people were amazed, for Ernest's face had come to perfectly resemble the face on the mountain. The virtues and goodness reflected in the great stone face had become embodied in the man who had modeled his life after that he had admired.[110]

Practice

When I was a missionary, a traveling elder, I used to roust the missionaries out of bed and have them recite three times with me, each time progressively louder: "Act enthusiastic and you'll be enthusiastic!" After the last time, we would all leap into the air, clap our hands, and exclaim, "Boy, am I enthusiastic!"

Sounds hokey, doesn't it? But aside from the elders looking at me as if I'd lost my mind and their feeling a little foolish, the acting out of enthusiasm actually produced enthusiasm. It's remarkable how our behavior shapes our attitudes as much as the other way around. And, indeed, this idea has scriptural basis. As John wrote, "Let no man deceive you: he that doeth righteousness is righteous, even as He is righteous" (1 John 3:7).

Dr. Willard Gaylin, professor of clinical psychiatry at Columbia University, once made the following observation:

> Kurt Vonnegut has said: "You are what you pretend to be, which is simply another way of saying you are what we (all of us) perceive you to be, not what you think you are."
>
> Consider for a moment the case of the 90-year-old man on his deathbed (surely the Talmud must deal with this?), joyous and relieved over the success of his

deception. For 90 years he has shielded his evil nature from public observation. For 90 years he has affected courtesy, kindness, and generosity—suppressing all the malice he knew was within him, while he calculatedly and artificially substituted grace and charity. All his life he had been fooling the world into believing he was a good man. This "evil" man will, I predict, be welcomed into the Kingdom of Heaven.

Similarly, I will not be told that the young man who earns his pocket money by mugging old ladies is "really" a good boy. Even my generous and expansive definition of goodness will not accommodate that particular form of self-advancement.

It does not count that beneath the rough exterior he has a heart—or, for that matter, an entire innards—of purest gold, locked away from human perception. You are for the most part what you seem to be, not what you would wish to be, nor, indeed, what you believe yourself to be.[111]

The truth is, what we enact, we become.

Priorities

Putting things in the proper order, getting first what ought to be first. When I mentioned the pictures on my walls, I did not mention the most important one—the visage of Christ. Christianity is not summarized in a set of rules or a philosophical system but in the life and mission of an individual—Jesus Christ. As He said, "I am the way, the truth, and the life: no man cometh unto the Father, but by me" (John 14:6). And of the Nephites, He asked, "What manner of men ought ye to be?" and answered,

"Verily, I say unto you, even as I am" (3 Nephi 27:27). Seeking to emulate the life of the divine hero, the ultimate personification of goodness, Jesus Christ, not pursuing some abstract list of virtues, is the key to our becoming better than we are.

Christ commanded us to seek first the kingdom of God and later noted that the kingdom of God is within each of us (see Matthew 6:33). The establishment of the kingdom of God on earth depends on finding and bringing forth that kingdom that is within ourselves. This comes by freely submitting our will to that of Christ and following His pattern.

The call of Christ to the rich young man to sell all that he had, give to the poor, and follow Him, is in fact a call to all of us. We also need to give up those things that we esteem but that are holding us back from truly accepting Christ as our Savior. Our worldly riches or treasures may include our way of life, our material possessions, our bad habits, practices that dull our senses, our friends whom we follow to win acceptance and praise, and certain forms of music and entertainment that degrade. All those things to which we are so addicted, that we cannot give up for His sake, these are our riches and define the allegiance of our hearts. And, like the rich young man, when the call is made to give up all our riches, many of us, too, may depart from Him sorrowing—sorrowing because we will never achieve all that He has offered us.

Christ saves us not only from the finality of death but from our separation from God. We are in one sense separated from God by our failure to develop the God-like traits that would make us resemble Him. Until we grow into the image of God within us, we will be unable to see Him or be with Him. This is what the apostle was teaching us when he wrote: "Beloved, now are we the sons of God, [but] it doth not yet appear what we shall be: but we know that, when he shall appear, we shall be like him; for we shall see him as he is. And every man that hath this hope in him purifieth himself, even as he is pure" (1 John 3:2–3).

Our liberation from the shackles that prevent us from becoming better than we are depends on giving up our "riches" and following Him. Those riches that impede us from becoming better than we are, are called sins. Again, as John observed, "Whosoever abideth in him sinneth not: whosoever sinneth hath not seen him, neither known him" (1 John 3:6).

Prayer

I believe we often underestimate the true power of prayer. The most critical aspect of prayer is to see the world and, most important, ourselves as God sees it and us. Insofar as our mortal limitations allow, we need to see, to picture, as He views, not from the limited perspective of this time, this moment, this place, or this situation, but to see in totality, all at once. Paul referred to us having the "mind of Christ" (1 Corinthians 2:16), and the Lord said to Joseph Smith that "He who hath faith to see shall see" (D&C 42:49). We are often chained by time, place, and circumstance. We need to pray always that we may see ourselves, if perhaps still obscurely, as He sees us so that we may understand and meet the requirements of what we need to do to realize the possibilities within.

Persistence

In the movement toward becoming better than we are, I would mention *Persistence* as the last "P." We need to serve Him and, therefore, give the best within ourselves in good times and in bad. As Peter observed, "Wherefore gird up the loins of your mind, be sober, and hope to the end for the grace that is to be brought unto you at the revelation of Jesus Christ; As obedient children, not fashioning yourself according to the former lusts in your ignorance: But as he which hath called you is holy, so be ye holy" (1 Peter 1:13–15). A contemporary rendering of Peter's words may clarify further what the Lord's chief apostle was saying: "You must therefore be mentally stripped for action, perfectly self-controlled. Fix your hopes on the gift of grace which is to be yours when Jesus Christ is revealed. As obedient children, do not let your character be shaped any longer by the desires you cherished in your days of ignorance. The One who called you is holy; like him, be holy in all your behavior, because Scripture says, 'You shall be holy, for I am holy'" (1 Peter 1:13–16, NEB).

Quest

This striving to be better than we are, to become that for which we are destined, to grow into our divine sonship and daughtership, to become even as Christ is—this is the great "Q," the "Quest" of life. This is the holy grail. The quest of life is not to *get* somewhere but to *become* someone.

We should measure our progress, our sanctification, not by reference to others but by reference to our potential and to our individual submission to Him who is the author and finisher of our faith and salvation, Jesus Christ the Son of the living God. While rejoicing in our present blessings and accomplishments, let us humbly reach beyond them.

There is in this quest no easy optimism but rather, divine hope. Some see the "can do" optimism and "true grit" attitudes of earlier ages, such as the Victorian age and the early part of the twentieth century, as too superficial and too smug. This was the period of the Horatio Alger books and the tales of Little Orphan Annie. If that earlier optimism seems to many to be too facile, I would nonetheless argue that there was real wisdom in that hopefulness, for it emphasized noble possibilities, energetic commitment, and personal responsibility. By contrast our age often seems to celebrate failure, low aspirations, unworthy and superficial goals, and death in the midst of life. It is ironic that our generation far surpasses earlier human epochs in the possession of material comforts, but we seem to have more individual and collective unhappiness than one would have thought, given these more favorable circumstances. The most noticeable noise emanating from too many contemporary Americans may be that of whining. I fear, alas, that earlier Americans may be our superiors in seeing the possibilities and in realizing that all resources and all technology are but tools in the quest of becoming better than we are.

If there is any defect in the self-improvement approaches of Horatio Alger and Little Orphan Annie, it is not in seeing possibilities but in not understanding the real limitations in realizing those possibilities through utter self-reliance. Ultimately, all things are indeed possible, but in the Lord—that is, through our willingness to submit to Christ and to allow the Holy Ghost to strive with us unto sanctification.

Illuminated by the Light of Christ and led by the Holy Spirit, the great journey of life is one of discovery—of finding who we really are and in becoming that person. There is a Hindu tale told of the supreme god of all the gods wishing to punish men for their inattention, sloth, and ignobility. He decided to hide from mankind that divine spark that had been given to humans and had always been visible. Some of the gods proposed hiding the divine spark in the ground, others suggested the top of a great mountain, still others on the moon, but in every case, the supreme god noted that man would some day burrow in the earth, scale the mountains, and even walk upon the moon. He concluded:

"We will hide their divinity deep in the center of their own being, for humans will never think to look for it there."[112] Indeed, much of life seems contrived to prevent us from looking there. Enlightened by Him who is our master, we must, however, look there, and we must follow the way that the Master has traced. When we pass beyond the veil, all our possessions and ambitious projects will be left behind. We will take with us only who we have become. Let us then strive without fail to become better than we are.

There was once a farmer named Hafed, who lived in ancient Persia. He was visited by a mystic from the East who told him that located throughout the world were vast stores of diamonds. Only a handful would make a man rich beyond belief, and possessing an entire mine, he could rule the world. Enchanted by such a fabulous prospect, Hafed sold his farm and all his possessions, left his family, and went in search of such diamonds. After years of fruitless searching and having exhausted his resources, he died a pauper, alone in a strange land. Many years later another Persian was digging in Hafed's now-deserted garden and discovered the diamond mines of Golconda, the richest of the ancient world.[113] Our possibilities and our happiness do not lie at great distances but are already at hand.

Quietude

The final "Q" is the blessed state of those whose quest is in a life of betterment through the ennobling pictures in their minds, their daily practice of righteousness, their well-ordered priorities, their revelatory prayers, and their persistence. This beatific "Q" is "Quietude" or peace. Like Christ, we may grow from grace to grace and in so doing, discover that all anxiety is, as Thomas à Kempis wrote, but vanity—worthless, trivial, and pointless.[114] So focused and so touched by grace, we will hear in our minds and feel in our hearts the ultimate blessing pronounced by the mortal Messiah: "Peace I leave with you, my peace I give unto you: not as the world giveth, give I unto you. Let not your heart be troubled, neither let it be afraid" (John 14:27).

May this be our lot.

ENDNOTES

1. John Keegan, *The Face of Battle* (New York: Penguin Books, 1978).
2. Brigham Young, *Discourses of Brigham Young,* sel. John A. Widtsoe (Salt Lake City: Deseret Book Company, 1954), 284.
3. Plato, *The Republic, Plato: The Complete Works* (Indianapolis, Cambridge: Hackett Publishing Company, 1997), Book VIII:544.
4. Ibid., Part IV, Books VIII–IX.
5. Ibid., Book VIII:562–64.
6. *The Landmark Thucydides* (New York: Touchstone Book, 1998), 3:82–84.
7. Neal A. Maxwell, *The Promise of a Brighter Day* (Salt Lake City: Deseret Book, 2001), 82.
8. Gordon B. Hinckley, in Conference Report, October 2001, 4.
9. Gordon B. Hinckley, "The Dawning of a Brighter Day," *Ensign,* May 2004, 81.
10. "The Morning Breaks," in *Hymns of The Church of Jesus Christ of Latter-day Saints* (Salt Lake City: The Church of Jesus Christ of Latter-day Saints, 1985), no. 1.
11. "The Spirit of God," *Hymns,* no. 2.
12. Gordon B. Hinckley, in Conference Report, October 2001, 4.
13. See Karen Lynn Davidson, *Our Latter-Day Hymns: The Stores and the Messages* (Salt Lake City: Bookcraft, 1988), 393–94.
14. John Jaques, "Oh Say, What Is Truth?" *Hymns,* no. 272.

15. Boyd K. Packer, First Worldwide Leadership Training Meeting, 11 January 2003.

16. *New York Times,* 5 June 1998.

17. See Joseph Smith, *Lectures on Faith* (Salt Lake City: Deseret Book Company, 1985), 67–71.

18. See John Jaques, "Oh Say, What Is Truth?" *Hymns,* no. 272.

19. Moses Maimonides, *Guide to the Perplexed, in Medieval Political Philosophy,* ed. Ralph Lerner and Muhsin Mahdi (New York: The Free Press, 1963).

20. Cited by M. Littleton, in *Moody Monthly* (Chicago: Moody Publishers, June 1989), 29.

21. Robert Frost, "Neither out Far Nor in Deep," *The Poetry of Robert Frost* (New York: Henry Holt and Company, 1979), 301.

22. Joseph Smith, *Lectures on Faith,* 7, 12.

23. C. S. Lewis, *The Last Battle,* in *The Chronicles of Narnia* (New York: HarperCollins Publishers, 1956), 742–48.

24. C. S. Lewis, *The Magician's Nephew,* in ibid., 98.

25. Neal A. Maxwell, *We Talk of Christ, We Rejoice in Christ* (Salt Lake City: Deseret Book Company, 1984), 93.

26. John Henry Newman, "Lead, Kindly Light," *Hymns,* no. 97.

27. C. S. Lewis, *The Great Divorce and The Problem of Pain,* in *The Complete C. S. Lewis* (San Francisco: HarperSanFrancisco, 2002), 340, 420.

28. John Milton, *Paradise Lost* (New York: Barnes and Noble Classics, 2004), 4:75.

29. Recounted by President Henry D. Moyle to the author while serving as a missionary in the France Mission, 1958.

30. Neal A. Maxwell, *All These Things Shall Give Thee Experience* (Salt Lake City: Deseret Book Company, 2007), 23.

31. Socrates, *Apology,* in *Plato: Complete Works,* ed. John M. Cooper (Indianapolis/Cambridge: Hackett Publishing Company, 1997), 21.

32. Abraham J. Heschel, *The Insecurity of Freedom: Essays on Human Existence* (Philadelphia: Jewish Publication Society, 1966), 4–5.

33. David O. McKay, *Gospel Ideals* (Salt Lake City: Deseret Book Company, 1953), 390.

34. C. S. Lewis, *The Screwtape Letters,* in *The Complete C. S. Lewis* (San Francisco: HarperSanFrancisco, 2002), 143.

35. David O. McKay, *Gospel Ideals* (Salt Lake City: Deseret Book Company, 1953), 390–91.

36. John Jaques, "Oh Say, What Is Truth?" *Hymns,* no. 272.

37. Plato, *The Republic,* in *Plato: Complete Works,* ed. John M. Cooper (Indianapolis/Cambridge: Hackett Publishing Company, 1997), Books II, III, X.

38. Kurt Cobain, "Serve the Servants," from *In Utero,* Geffin Records, 1993.

39. Charles W. Penrose, "School Thy Feelings," *Hymns,* 336.

40. David O. McKay, in Conference Report, September–October 1950, 108–9.

41. John Nicholson, "Come, Follow Me," *Hymns,* no. 116.

42. Elder Richard L. Evans cited this statement of Lowell Thomas at the author's high school graduation in June 1955. It impressed him then and since.

43. Thornton Wilder, *Our Town* (New York: Harper and Brothers, 1957), 60.

44. Brigham Young, *Discourses of Brigham Young,* 82–83.

45. Ibid., 69.

46. Ibid.

47. Parley P. Pratt, "Do What Is Right," *Hymns,* no. 237.

48. C. S. Lewis, *The Voyage of the Dawn Treader,* in *The Chronicles of Narnia* (New York: HarperCollins Publishers, 1956), 473, 475.

49. Albert Einstein, in *The Data Administration Newsletter,* November 2–8, 2003; www.tdan.com/quotes.htm (accessed 2/21/07).

50. J.K. Rowling, *Harry Potter and the Chamber of Secrets* (New York: Scholastic and Lantern Design, 2000), 333.

51. Robert Bolt, *A Man for All Seasons* (New York: Vintage Books, 1990), 65.

52. Alan Jay Lerner and Frederick Loewe, *Camelot* (produced and opened in New York City, 3 December 1960, Tam Witmark, production rights).

53. *The Basic Works of Aristotle,* ed. Richard McKeon (New York: The Modern Library, 2001), *Physica,* II.1, 192b32.3; *Ethica Nicomachea,* I.1; *Politica,* I.2.

54. Bill Watterson, *The Calvin and Hobbes–Tenth Anniversary Book* (Kansas City: Andrews and McMeel, 1995), 105.

55. William Shakespeare, *Macbeth,* in *The Yale Shakespeare* (New York: Barnes and Noble, 2005), 3.14.111–112.

56. Ibid., 5.5.27–29.

57. Alexander Pope, *Essay on Man,* in *The Major Works* (New York: Oxford University Publishing, 2006), 2.5.217–220.

58. David O. McKay, in Conference Report, October 1968, 86.

59. William Fowler, "We Thank Thee, O God, for a Prophet," *Hymns,* no. 19.

60. Richard Whately, in *The Oxford Dictionary of Quotations* (London: Oxford University Press, 1955), 565.

61. John Patrick, *Teahouse of the August Moon,* based on the novel by Vern Sneider (New York: Dramatic Play Service, Inc., 1957), Act 1, Scene i, 6.

62. Miguel de Cervantes. www.quoteworld.org/quotes/2567 (accessed 2/21/07).

63. John Milton, *Paradise Lost* (New York: Barnes and Noble Classics, 2004), 4:75.

64. Joseph Smith, *Teachings of the Prophet Joseph Smith,* sel. Joseph Fielding Smith (Salt Lake City: Deseret Book Company, 1976), 298.

65. Charles M. de Talleyrand said this at the news of the murder of the Duc d'Engien. www.thinkexist.com (accessed 2/22/07).

66. Jane Stanford, 1828–1905, wife of Leland Stanford.

67. Jean de la Bruyere. www.theabsolute.net/minefield/pwords.html (accessed 2/22/07).

68. Plutarch, *Essays* (New York: Penguin Books, 1992), 42.

69. Ibid., 234.

70. Joseph Smith, *Teachings of the Prophet Joseph Smith,* 255.

71. Eliza R. Snow, "O My Father," *Hymns,* no. 292.

72. William Wordsworth, "Ode: Intimations of Immortality," in Margaret Ferguson, Mary Ho Salter, and Jon Stallsworthy, *The Norton Anthology of Poetry* (New York: W. W. Norton and Co., 2005), 796–98.

73. Ibid., 799.

74. Stuart K. Hine, "How Great Thou Art," *Hymns,* no. 86.

75. Joseph Smith, *Teachings of the Prophet Joseph Smith,* 256.

76. Boethius, *The Consolation of Philosophy* (New York: Penquin Books, 1969), 113–15.

77. Ibid.

78. *Church News,* 30 December 1989.

79. Francis Bacon, in Tyron Edwards, *The New Dictionary of Thoughts,* revised and enlarged by C. N. Catravas and Jonathan Edwards (New York: Standard Book Co., 1955), 565.

80. Henry Ward Beecher, in ibid., 114.

81. C. S. Lewis, *The Weight of Glory and Other Addresses* (New York: Touchstone, 1996), 19.

82. Thomas Carlyle, in Tyron Edwards, *The New Dictionary of Thoughts,* 565.

83. Joseph Fielding Smith, *Doctrines of Salvation,* comp. Bruce R. McConkie, 3 vols. (Salt Lake City: Deseret Book, 2004), 2:35–37.

84. Bruce R. McConkie, *The Promised Messiah* (Salt Lake City: Deseret Book Company, 1978), 553.

85. This talk was given in the Assembly Hall in 1985. President Boyd K. Packer returned to this theme in his October 1997 general conference address, "Called to Serve."

86. John Milton, *The Complete Poems* (New York: Penguin Books, 2004), 40.

87. Sir Philip Sidney, *Selected Prose and Poetry*, ed. Robert Kimbrough (Madison: University of Wisconsin Press, 1983), 359.

88. Francis Bacon, in Tyron Edwards, *The New Dictionary of Thoughts*, 250.

89. Earl Philip Chesterfield, in ibid., 251.

90. Edward George Bulwer-Lytton, in ibid., 250.

91. Earl Philip Chesterfield, in ibid.

92. Rudyard Kipling, "God of Our Fathers, Known of Old," *Hymns*, no. 80.

93. Terrance D. Olson, "The Morality of Emotions," in *Meridian Magazine*, 5 February 2001, 94–95.

94. Spencer W. Kimball, *Teachings of Spencer W. Kimball*, ed. Edward L. Kimball (Salt Lake City: Bookcraft, 1985), 135.

95. Howard W. Hunter, "Reading the Scriptures," *Ensign*, November 1979, 64.

96. President Gordon B. Hinckley mentioned this in a meeting with other General Authorities.

97. Joseph Smith, *Lectures on Faith*, 2–4.

98. "Know This, That Every Soul Is Free," *Hymns*, no. 240.

99. Joseph Smith, quoted by John Taylor, "The Organization of the Church," *Millennial Star* 15, November 1851, 339.

100. John Locke, *A Letter Concerning Toleration*, trans. William Popple, www.Constitution.org/jl/tolerati.htm (accessed 2/21/07).

101. James Madison, *Memorial and Remonstrance against Religious Assessments*, The Founders' Constitution, Volume 5, Amendment I (Religion), Document 43. http://press-pubs.uchicago.edu/founders/print_documents/amendI_religions43.html (accessed 3/21/07).

102. www. wikipedia.org/wiki/Novus_Ordo_Seclorum (accessed 3/21/07).

103. For the definitive analysis of Lincoln's political thought, see Harry V. Jaffa, *Crisis of the House Divided* (Chicago: University of Chicago Press, 1959, 1982), and *A New Birth of Freedom* (New York: Rowman and Littlefield Publishers, Inc., 2000).

104. Alexis de Tocqueville, *Democracy in America*, ed. Thomas Bender (New York: Modern Library, 1981), 185.

105. Thomas Jefferson, *Jefferson's Writings,* ed. Merrill D. Peterson (New York: Literary Classics of the United States, Inc., 1984), 4:289.

106. "The Family: A Proclamation to the World," *Ensign,* November 1995, 102.

107. Blaise Pascal, in Tyron Edwards, *The New Dictionary of Thoughts,* 196.

108. Joseph Smith, *Lectures on Faith,* 7, 12.

109. Jimmy Van Heusen and Johnny Burke, "Swinging on a Star," in *Going My Way,* motion picture, 1944.

110. Nathaniel Hawthorne, *The Great Stone Face: And Other Tales of the White Mountains* (West Valley City, Utah: Waking Lion Press, 2006), 1–32.

111. Willard Gaylin, *The New York Times,* 7 October 1977, A31.

112. "Quotes and Quips," in *Hinduism Today,* July/August/September 2005; www.hinduismtoday.com/archives/2005/7–9/14–15_quips.shtml (accessed 2/21/07).

113. Based on Russell H. Conwell, *Acres of Diamonds* (New York: Harper and Brother, 1915), 3–62.

114. Thomas à Kempis, *The Imitation of Christ* (New York: Penguin Books, 1952), 27–28.

INDEX

INDEX